The PAIN of BEING HUMAN

Eugene Kennedy

The PAIN of BEING HUMAN

NEW, REVISED EDITION

A Crossroad Book
The Crossroad Publishing Company
New York

1997

The Crossroad Publishing Company
370 Lexington Avenue, New York, NY 10017

Printed in the United States of America

Library of Congress Cataloging-in-Publication Data
Kennedy, Eugene C.
    The pain of being human / Eugene Kennedy.
       p. cm.
    "New revised edition of the million-copy bestseller."
    ISBN 0-8245-1682-6 (pbk.)
    1. Conduct of life. I. Title.
BF637.C5K46 1997
158 – dc21
                                   97-29515
                                       CIP

For
Jack and Rosemary Muratori
loving friends of a lifetime

CONTENTS

Preface

BEING IMPERFECT
WITH GRACE

V ISITING A BOOK written long ago resembles opening King Tut's tomb. Planning only to rid it of references so old that they need carbon dating, the writer unwittingly frees spirits with ideas of their own. Reseal the tomb immediately, they insist, or excavate it completely, exorcise its curses, and refit it for new times.

So the book, extensively rewritten — much of it new material — has changed greatly. So, too, have the circumstances of life in the post-modern, pre-millennial world. Being human, however, remains the same. When we read that the bier for a sixty-thousand-year-old hide-wearing hunter ancestor had been spread with spring flowers, we suddenly notice our family resemblance. The Neanderthal's otherness disappears; we can almost smell the garlands and feel the hands that place them now in our imagination as gently as they did once beneath the body of their beloved.

This tender gesture bespeaks love, loss, and longing that we all feel. These are some of the pains of our being human. Every generation, whether called Lost, Post-War, Boomers, or X, must deal with these reminders of how much, despite publicized differences, we are all alike, or how truly we belong to the same family.

Mothers warn their children about many things, but they cannot prepare them, except in general, for their inevitable encounters with the limitations of the human condition. These include aging and mortality, illness, tangled emotional involvements, big things like broken relationships and little ones like everyday hurts.

This is a book of meditations on dealing with the things mothers could not warn us about and for which nobody could really prepare us but with which we must all deal. Beneath the bravado, Hemingway tried to warn us about the ordinary pains of life that he felt so keenly. The revelatory experience through which we lose

11

our innocence is not, however, killing a man in a battle or a bull in a corrida, nor even sexual initiation. It is rather our discovery of our structural imperfection, the basic element of the mystery of being human.

From this fundamental imperfection arise our possibilities — there would be no love, no courage, no curiosity were perfection possible — along with our greatest failures and disappointments. If Hemingway wrote famously of courage as grace under pressure, these meditations concern something more common and certain in our experience: Being imperfect with grace in everyday life.

A Few Words of Thanks

Let me begin with Michael Leach, who proposed this revision to me. His insight and enthusiasm gladden the heart and substantially reduce the pain of being published.

Ms. Cynthia Baines deserves great credit for so patiently transforming my prescription-style handwriting into a finely typed manuscript. She made it seem like fun.

It is fortunate that my wife, Sara Charles, M.D., is a psychiatrist. She understands that, in order to do their work, writers must be generally distractable and, indeed, go a little harmlessly mad each day and must be gently helped to reconstruct themselves by dinner time.

I am grateful that Mrs. Lois Wallace represents me with friendship, good humor, and a practical judgment that is never ambiguous.

Lastly, I would remember my old friend, Joseph Cardinal Bernardin of Chicago, with whom I spent a great deal of time while rewriting this book. Dying of cancer, he understood and bravely transformed his pain into spiritual growth. That example made millions of us more courageous in accepting our daily pains of being human.

Chapter 1

"OUR" PAIN, OURSELVES

T ASTING THE BITTERNESS of this almost spent century, we have come to associate pain almost exclusively with sickness, loss, or our own inhumanity. The signature of pain is written large on suffering faces: the shrunken native children whose crusted lids cannot hide their thousand-year-old eyes; the tragic surprise on the faces of the concentration camp victims in their final experience of deception in the gas chambers; the desperate look of the dying hospital patient searching us for hope we cannot give.

There is, however, another kind of pain in life that has nothing to do with sickness or our sometime savagery. This is the suffering of healthy persons, as undramatic as it is inevitable, as commonplace as it is uncomforted. It is the pain with a thousand private faces, the pain that comes from just being human.

No antidote exists for the ache of our struggle to become ourselves as human beings and children of God. Money cannot buy it off, luxuries do not soften it, and not even the Concorde travels fast or far enough to outdistance it. Nor is escape possible through surfing on the Internet, Twelve Step plans, diets, or workouts with a personal trainer. "There is no cure for Autumn," John Cheever tells us, "no medicine for the North wind."

We cannot run away from this pain without running away from ourselves. We are ashamed of it only if we misunderstand it. We can dull our perception of it in a hundred ways, but that makes the meaning of life float, like an astronaut's cup, just beyond our grasp. F. Scott Fitzgerald, born in St. Paul, Minnesota, once described Midwestern snow as "our" snow. In the same way, this existential pain is "our" pain, the proof of our being human together. This is the pain that nobody could tell you about beforehand.

"Our" pain is just the right way to speak about the subject. The revolution in the study of pain that has taken place over the last generation validates the idea that we humans suffer pain in a far more complex way than was once supposed. Pain is no longer regarded mechanically, a harmful stimulus causing "tissue damage" transmitted through the nervous system to the brain as automatically and indifferently as a power surge through house wiring to a computer disk.

In that old model, you either had real pain from "tissue damage" or it was all in your head. Now scientists understand that pain is highly personal, that, according to the International Association for the Study of Pain, it is "an unpleasant sensory *and emotional* experience." Researchers emphasize that pain must be understood not only as an "emotional experience" but as "always subjective." David B. Morris observes that "human subjectivity cannot somehow be washed out as an impure and undesirable variant in the analysis of pain."*

In other words, it is not all in our heads; it is "us" expressing ourselves, telling our brains who we are, where we have been, whether we love or are loved, what we believe — the mystery of ourselves engraved as bold as braille. It is sensitive to the touch because it bears the message not only of a current hurt but the memory of all our hurts.

Pain speaks for our total personalities, our cultural experience, and our relationships with each other. Pain is as personal as politics are said to be local. Through it we write our signature on our existence. Sometimes we need help to make it out. For pain must be read as music, painting, literature, or dance are: revelations from the depths of our unique mystery. "Our" pain holds, as its rings do the history of a tree, the story of our being human.

Our pain is then too precious and too profound in its meaning to be oversimplified as tissue damage and nothing more. Our suffering is, in a way that we are just beginning to grasp, a tender portal to our souls. Each person's suffering is different, each a transcendent signal, each, then, a statement less about the pain than about the man or woman suffering it. It must be approached, as everything sacred must, with reverence and a measure of awe.

Healthy persons do not experience their struggle to be human as passive victims to the nameless fates. In entering and embracing the normal pain of life they discover their own inner strength

---

*David B. Morris, "Pain's Dominion: What We Make of Pain," *Wilson Quarterly* (Autumn 1994): 8–26.

to be free and responsible. As great and graceful pottery emerges from fire, our best selves come out only when we experience the truth about our inescapable frustrations and longings. This happens when we sense throughout ourselves that, set in the field of time and space, the human condition is by its nature imperfect and limited. We absorb this defining truth about ourselves as we do the environment — seaside, big city, or farmland — of our childhood. It becomes inseparable from our personal identity, and we sense it whenever we wonder, in whatever situation, whether we can make it or not.

In this rich soil we dig deep for the meaning of faith and hope, virtues that come to life when we are keenly aware of our incomplete and struggling situation. Indeed, this quite ordinary effort to believe in ourselves and in others makes us one in the human condition. If shedding each other's blood makes us enemies, sharing each other's tears makes us brothers and sisters. We men and women are linked to one another, like mountain climbers on a steep ascent, in the common struggle to grow and be wise, to learn and to love.

The deepest nerves of life are touched in our relationships with each other. We feel them in moments of misunderstanding, in the uneasy times, for example, when a friend demands a loyalty that would make us untrue to ourselves. We feel it when we cannot seem to break through to another and, feeling isolated, are left alone with a personal grief as much a part of us as an open wound. Pain is present when we face freedom's choices and we are not at all sure what the right course will be either for ourselves or for others. Pain is there whenever we are challenged really to trust someone else and we are really afraid to do it. That is always the real price of trust, so easily spoken of and so hard to bestow. Such everyday suffering deepens and changes but never really lessens as we become more aware of our dangerous responsibility for our humanity.

Anybody who is really alive recognizes this anguish as the prime test of existence. It is compounded of hurt feelings and unfulfilled dreams, of heads dizzied by the climb on the bridge of change that ascends into the mists hanging over a new century, and hearts scarred by the efforts to live truly and courageously every day.

Fear crackles like fire in every life, fed by the uncertainties that are a constant part of people and events. Small wonder that we dream universally of desert islands, of quiet safe places where we might catch our breath for a moment. But there are no such islands, not for any of us. There is only life, unfolding quite mysteriously and with ever-present challenge even in the most commonplace existences.

This is the truth about life that impatient youth, feeling immortal and ever determined to undo the sins of the just past generation, find difficult to understand. They are shocked to be bloodied by coming upon it as if unaware. After nothing but victories, they may lose something big and taste it for the first time. Even those most anxious to encourage the visions of the young cannot shield them from the moment in which they inevitably face their own personal test with real life. It is easy to be brave before this moment comes. But life waits for all of us very patiently. Nobody is exempt from the faulted human conditions forever. It is much harder to go on being brave after the first real moment of truth comes into one's life. Part of the pain of life for parents lies in the fact that they cannot protect their children from life. No mother can warn them sufficiently or hope even to be understood if she tries. Nor can she suffer for them. Parents can only do their best and set their children free to encounter existence on their own.

What life is really all about flows from the simple experiences of what we are like with those we love. There is no life except in relationship to others, be they spouses, friends, children or pupils, parishioners or chance acquaintances. Lovers who know the only experience that transcends time and space also know a lot about suffering. If they never taste the pain of loving, they are never really lovers at all. The more deeply and truly people love, by that measure they also know the suffering that is the lining of all love.

There are separations and goodbyes, and tests for lovers growing old and staying in love, the challenges to be faithful and responsible to each other even as life alters them and their circumstances. What nourishes the love of a man and woman long after they are as familiar with the inner folds and wrinkles of each other's faults and failings as a blind man with the walls of home? What sustains a wife's responsible love for her husband when he is no longer a hero on a white charger in her eyes? What keeps her faithful to him after she knows he will never keep his promises of setting the world on fire, or even getting that long sought promotion? So too, something deeper than romance keeps a man responsible for his wife even after she is no longer young or as beautiful as she once seemed in his eyes. How do they look at each other and still see their long lost fairness and beauty? Lovers find faith and hope only as they face pain together, the pain that is never completely dulled, the pain that is not an impurity but an essential part of the precious metal of love.

This pain is part of every lover's longing and is not diminished but rather heightened by the realization that, in this life, they can never share each other or anything else completely. So lovers rely on each other in a trial of faith and trust that is never over and done with. They understand hope because they constantly make themselves vulnerable through believing in one another. Real lovers never escape the pain of life, but they do conquer the restlessness that betrays the unloving and the unloved. They find peace, and it passes all understanding, because they realize that suffering and dying are not enemies but necessary conditions for real living.

Here we discover the glowing core of the ordinary pain of being human. We learn to yield ourselves up, saying yes to life by saying yes to each other, or we hide from each other and, instead of love, harvest alienation and despair. There is a dying that goes into living with others, a daily surrender of the self for which there is no substitute. For believers this is not just a philosophy saying that you must pay for what you get in life. The "spiritual life" is an unfortunately abstract phrase that may suggest that God's grace touches only some higher and better part of ourselves, or that it is lived only in moments of detachment from the human condition, on distant mountain tops, in desert remove or in places of pilgrimage where we may conquer "our" pain briefly and think we have become spiritual at last.

The life of the spirit, however, is lived back in the noisy, broken world of our ordinary lives with each other. The readiness to die in reaching out in love involves us in the mystery of suffering that is an integral part of every real religion. This demands a crucifixion, not just a reluctant carrying while we curse our crosses. The pain of being human is not something we are merely called to put up with. Living in the spirit, we are redeemed and redeem each other through our active acceptance of everything that an ordinary human life entails, small deaths to ourselves at every turn. These lead directly to resurrection because as these deaths are embraced

they generate life in us that is bright and warm enough to give life
to others.

There is a great deal of talk about the risk involved in loving.
This is not, however, a risk that means the outcome will be either
painful or pleasurable for us. Suffering is, in fact, guaranteed for
anyone who takes on the task of loving. Persons who love will
suffer, but they will also find a fullness of life and a personal experience of the Spirit's presence. "What the Spirit brings," St. Paul
wrote to the Galatians, "is very different" from the tangled emotions that the self-indulgent and self-conscious inherit. The Spirit
brings "love, joy, peace, patience, kindness, goodness, trustfulness,
gentleness, and self-control." These virtues blossom only out of the
soil of our relationships with each other: they are the first fruits of
committing ourselves to the ordinary pains in our daily struggle
to love. There is no setting in which these can have any meaning
outside of sharing life with each other in the human condition.

Humans are made strong enough to face hard truths. The hardest is that the healthiest of us come alive only when we are able to
understand and affirm that we will always live with pain. Stoicism
never makes this truth really bearable. Cynicism makes it completely intolerable. The heart of a spiritual life lies not in rules or
rituals, nor in the magic remaking of a difficult world. Persons of
faith face the inexorable truth that we find life only when we are
realistic enough to let ourselves lose it as we seek to love others.
Utopia is not a guiding vision. There is no airy Camelot for persons who open themselves to the deepest reality of life's struggle.
We are not persons or spiritual until we understand the pain of being human, "our" pain, the pain of all our woe and wonder, of our
groundedness in time when we are made for the eternal.

Chapter 2

THE WORST THING ABOUT
THE PAIN OF BEING HUMAN

THE WORST THING about the pain of being human is that it doesn't kill us; we never die of pain, although we sometimes wish that we could, if only to put an end to it. And the worst pains are those which seem to have no remedies, the ones that tear the edges of our spirit because they come when we are healthy rather than when we are sick. We may try to tranquilize these pains away, but eventually the ache returns. They even go on vacation with us, waiting for an idle moment or a familiar song to use as an entrance into our hearts.

What is this pain that will not kill us, this ache that has learned how to follow us so closely through life? It is the pain of being alive, the pain of always having to face a new challenge, the pain of wanting love (and the pain of finding it), the ache of starting again when we don't feel like it, the tension of coming to terms with a life that keeps shifting under our feet.

There are a lot of simple old cures for this kind of suffering, some of which we have forgotten in the midst of our fleeting friendships with mood adjustment and sleep aids, and in our ability to purchase a kind of friendship in psychotherapy. The oldest antidote is to shake ourselves loose from our passivity, to face down the inclination we have to play Camille in order to get a little sympathy from ourselves if not from the crowd around us.

Like the old country doctor's remedies, compounded from a wisdom that still endures, the old-fashioned idea of pulling ourselves together is not really half bad. Perhaps we have grown enamored, in late twentieth-century America, of brooding over the stresses of our lives, of counting liabilities more than blessings, of waiting for love rather than loving, of embracing victimhood and dependency in lives lived at a safe secondhand distance. In fact, actively loving may well be the key to a much better handling of the pain that hurts but does not kill. Giving, despite the hoarfrost of the cliché, still beats getting; it's about as therapeutic as anything we know. And if we are persistent, this course of treatment not only makes us feel better; it leads us to real loves as well.

The season of Lent has an old tradition of self-inflicted pain in behalf of the expansion of the spirit; those of us who are Christian once almost enjoyed forty days of purple and penance. That's all gone now; the spirit of Lent is doing something positive these days, and that, of course, is all to the good. But instead of trying to dull it, suppress it, or just avoid it, perhaps we could take on the source of our worst human ache instead of avoiding it or smoothing it over.

We might let ourselves feel it, and then organize ourselves so that this suffering no longer holds a secret kind of domination over our days. Some things, the poet tells us, are too deep for tears; but a real effort to do something positive might focus our attention on getting ourselves together enough to grow stronger in the face of the pain that is too cruel to kill us.

There are all kinds of things to do that help bring us out of ourselves and into a fuller life. This is not an invitation to stoic striving as much as a call to bolder, spiritual living. We can do more with our pain than suffer it, and the world needs lovers more than martyrs. The point is, of course, that the pain really won't kill us and that we should not let it keep us from reaching out to others just because that is the way we got hurt in the first place. You do not need Lent to do this. We can have another go at it any time; our pain will grow less as our hearts grow larger. We conquer the slow death of pain by a full try at life.

Chapter 3

HAPPINESS SEEMS
SIMPLE ENOUGH

H APPINESS is not too much to ask of life surely, not an excessive blessing to pray for, nor a grace beyond the powers above to grant to us. And yet it seems to be given only intermittently at best, and in small quantities at that. We spend more time seeking it and more energy stalking it than we do on almost anything else. There seems to be something wrong here, when so many people have so much difficulty achieving and holding on to the very thing they want most.

The inner nature of happiness is harder to unlock than that of the tiniest structure of nature. It goes along as a side-effect doing something noble and worthwhile and is not a commodity that can be directly sought and bought. And its heightened moments possess only a half-life; they pass quickly but they leave a deep and healing kind of peace behind in our hearts. "Happiness," as poet Robert Frost once wrote, "makes up in height for what it lacks in length."

But what, you ask, is the kind of worthy goal from which happiness is a spin-off? Probably the surest path to happiness, but one that is as narrow as the biblical way into heaven for a rich man, is through getting close to other persons. So often, however, that seems like turning one's back on happiness and opening a door to everybody's grief; it can mean a messy kind of involvement, an entangling kind of enterprise that throws chains around the heart that always hurt and sometimes break it. Because of these seeming terrors, we walk cautiously, sizing each other up like wary boxers. The way to stay content, we feel, or at least to stay safe, is to stay at a distance from others.

It is this kind of attitude toward others that generates alienation and loneliness, the twin specters that make people's hearts grow cold even while they are trying to buy or seduce a little happiness in one of the many ways the world says that it can be found. Their ambition often turns out to be a petty tyrant giving them little rest or happiness.

No, happy persons are those who work at being close to others in a respectful and loving way. They do not get close by taking but only by giving to others and learning then how to receive from them in turn. Happy people know that intimacy is not easy and that fidelity demands that they give themselves, undisguised and undefended, along with their word every day, to those they love.

Being close to others demands that we keep on learning both about ourselves and those we love. Most of all, it means that we prize others not as possessions but as other persons who need our freeing love to keep going in the way that is right for them in life. That is the love we read about in the Bible, the love that the Spirit gives us when we are brave enough, even when we don't think we are strong enough, to stick with others through the hazards of life.

Chapter 4

A THING OR TWO MORE ABOUT HAPPINESS

A T TIMES we make little of the biggest things in life in the hope that our uneasy laughter will hide our deep longing. So happiness has been described as a warm puppy, being famous, ice fishing, a faithful dog, and a day without phone calls. Even these examples point out two significant qualities of happiness: It may arise from quite ordinary experiences and it is very elusive.

These things are clues to our search for happiness, our alertness to finding it where we can, and our inability to hold on to it for very long.

Despite its importance for everybody, we do not have a very good definition of the experience of happiness. We can, however, unless we are completely numb to life, say whether we are happy or not. We have also learned something about the qualities of happiness.

Philosophers and literary men have grappled with the theme of happiness for centuries. Perhaps Goethe, in his version of *Faust,* has told us as much as any of them. In the familiar story, Dr. Faust, abandoning his scholarly but frustrating search for "truth," makes a pact with the devil. If the devil can deliver him to a moment of utter happiness that will cause him to say, "Stay, you are so beautiful," he will deliver his soul to the Prince of Darkness. The devil provides wine, women, and song in abundance. These afford pleasure but not happiness to Faust, and he is not moved to hold on to these experiences. Finally, as he looks from a hill at the successful outcome of a project to reclaim the land from the sea and as he hears the joyful sounds of children at play and observes men and women working hard in their homes and shops, Dr. Faust stakes a claim on the happy moment and speaks the fateful words. Most of us can identify with a similar experience of our own. We know the yearning to stop time in the instant of happiness even as we know the impossibility of doing so.

Happiness is filled with paradox. To get it, you must forget trying to grab at it directly. Happiness arises as a by-product of our becoming absorbed in something worthwhile outside ourselves. It is not necessarily correlated with pleasure. The world is filled with unhappy-looking millionaires and sad-looking yuppies. Even the merchants of pleasure seem a glum and lonely lot, constantly anxious about profit margins and competition.

Happiness is not passive, the product of the uneasy truces forged with the world through any chemical or erotic adventures that lead so often to tragedy. Passivity and withdrawal attract pain and violence rather than peace and contentment. Happy persons must be actively engaged with life despite its difficulties; there is no demilitarized zone of disengagement where happiness descends free of every human encumbrance.

Nor is happiness self-conscious. It flows from a life of purpose, especially one that is ordered to the service of others. Happiness is bound up with effort and struggle. That is why it shines in the lives of husbands and wives who strive to love each other and their children, even when they have mortgages and other troubles to deal with every day. Happiness does not live independently of sacrifice any more than real fulfillment of any kind does. The spiritual truth abides that persons ready to lose their lives truly find them, and this truth is the foundation of any real happiness. Individuals who strive to save their lives, to lay hold of happiness without letting go of themselves, are the ones who never find it at all.

A further paradox of happiness is that even those who experience it realize that they cannot hold on to it for very long. Life may have, as psychologist Abraham Maslow has put it, "peak moments," but these quietly and quickly dissolve and a more routine kind of feeling sets in. Happiness cannot be acquired once and for all in this life. A heightened feeling of contentment after a major accomplishment yields quickly as new tasks and new goals line up before us. Persons who acknowledge this are not frustrated, because a deeper wisdom tells them that happiness is not lost forever. Happiness returns as we recommit ourselves to the fresh challenge of life. One of the wiliest contemporary enemies of true happiness is the strong emphasis on immediate gratification and the inability of many people to postpone their satisfaction so that they can do the sometimes arduous work necessary for its attainment. Instant pleasure is our modern counterpart of the prodigal son's mess of pottage. For this reason wise persons have always spoken of the "pursuit of happiness," rightly emphasizing the purposeful life rather than daydreams of gold at the end of the rainbows and lottery drawings.

It is surely the task of every believer to see that the conditions necessary for happiness are available to everybody. Happiness is not made for one class or one skin color. Neither is it something that is reserved for the flawless who think they inherit the earth. Persons with great limitations can attain happiness through the very effort to overcome them. Many happy people deal with the reality of their problems and overcome them because of their faith and courage. That, however, is hard, not easy, work. The things that really make individuals happy are quite independent of wealth and circumstance. We can have them available anywhere if we sense the real meaning and values of life. Self-knowledge is, of course, indispensable to this understanding of happiness. People who know themselves do not set goals that are either beyond or beneath them. They constantly engage their strength in a realistic approach to tasks that match them. They do not demand what they can never achieve nor turn away from what they can really accomplish.

One price of happiness is that it is related to our capacity for deprivation. Persons who always have everything they think they want are not very happy at all. A continued exposure to anything, no matter how good or pleasurable, leads to satiety. Hunger, the old saying goes, is the best sauce. And this is true not only of physical things but also of the more profound and spiritual aspects of human experience.

Self-denial, a startling notion today unless connected with a work-out or health food for a better body, remains indispensable to the fulfillment that is a function of the spirit.

Even lovers must face separation at times. Constant togetherness can dull the deepest relationship. The joy of being reunited, the wonder of rediscovering each other: These are part of the happiness that is denied to persons who can never deny themselves. The latter individuals mistake security and a totally changeless world for the real meaning of happiness. But happiness flourishes on the shifting edge of life where people are ready for growth rather than a static and deceptive security. Happiness abhors a vacuum.

So, too, happiness comes when we are unselfconsciously ready to discipline ourselves in order to give our best effort in life. It flows from concentration and application of our fullest energies to the challenges that rise like the calendar pages before us. Being ourselves is a noble ideal, but it demands that we make the effort to be our best selves. This is far different from interpreting it as giving some kind of free rein to any and every impulse with the demand that others accept or "respect" us in return.

It is hard to beat the Beatitudes if one is really interested in the achievement of happiness. The Beatitudes have been translated in a manner that catches Christ's direct address to all those who would follow him. "How happy are the poor in spirit...happy the gentle...happy those who mourn...happy those who hunger and thirst for what is right...happy the merciful...the pure in heart...the peacemakers...." The accumulated wisdom of the ages has not improved on those words. We find happiness when we do not look directly for it but when we give ourselves over to others ready to face the pains and problems that do not destroy but, in a curious way, bind our contentment together.

Chapter 5

WHY DO WE ACT THIS WAY?
IT SUITS US

THE HUMAN RACE is proud of its historical progress, proud, for example, of the things that couldn't be done but that we ended up doing anyway, such as putting out the Kuwaiti oil fires quickly when doomsayers said that they would blacken the skies forever. Humans are also puzzled by the fact that, while they seem to want to move forward against the odds, they can also slide backward against their best interests and instincts. Human beings have wrung their hands and pounded their heads in regret at the wrong directions they take and that, strangely enough, they often take over again. Experience, they say, is the best teacher, but we frequently do not learn from it and, instead, go on repeating the same mistakes in our personal and public lives season after season.

A long list would not exhaust the examples of the perilous and self-defeating positions into which we constantly place ourselves. "Whatever you have, spend less," Samuel Johnson once urged, but in the age of easy credit, many find it almost necessary to do just the opposite. The resulting worry, the psychosomatic symptoms, and the slow contamination of the relationships we prize most are not enough to keep us from the temptations of piling up debt. Then there are those people, found in families, businesses, and even monasteries, who relate to each other by fighting constantly. Always upset and always irritated, they seem incapable of finding any other way of getting along.

The same is true of men and women who keep separating and coming back together again, missing each other when they are apart but knocking each other's brains out when they get together. Add to the list of those who keep doing things that get them into serious trouble even when they know full well what will happen to them because of it. Persons who always come late to work or who always drink just a little more than is good for them; those who complicate their already painful present by postponing important obligations to an indefinite future: These are some of the snags on which supposedly progressive people keep catching themselves. How does it all fit together and make any sense at all? Are these just random and mysterious aspects of human nature?

The reasons we do what we do can be very complex, but there are always reasons. Our behavior does not come out of nowhere and, with patience and insight, it can be traced down to its origins even when these are deep in our unconscious lives. Obviously, very tangled and complex motivation cannot be unraveled by amateur psychologists no matter how good-willed they may be. Many people need professional help in order to get to the real roots of the things they do to defeat themselves in daily life.

On the other hand, even reasonably mature and healthy people are frequently puzzled by why they do things that they know will hurt either themselves or other people. With a little reflection, or perhaps the ready ear of a good friend, we can all achieve a better understanding of our behavior and avoid at least some of our mistakes in the future.

One of the most helpful questions persons can ask when they are mystified by their own moods or actions is this: "What am I getting out of this anyway?" This question is helpful because we never do anything that does not reward us in one way or another. The reward need not be very obvious to be effective. It is just that we do not often inspect the dynamics of our day-to-day life and so we fail to appreciate the nature of many of the psychological transactions that we carry out with ourselves.

When, for example, our behavior causes us pain or embarrassment, a close look within ourselves may reveal that we are balancing the psychological books by punishing ourselves in some disguised way for something about which we feel guilty deep down inside. So too, we may discover that we endure certain punishing behavior, something as simple as drinking tonight even though we know we will be desperately ill tomorrow, because we want to seize the short-term gain, the comforting escape through alcohol, so that we need not look at the picture of our long-term responsibilities.

Why do we act this way? "It suits us" is the answer. Finding out why it suits us lights the path to real self-knowledge and self-acceptance.

The "why" leads us to ask other questions that bring us into corners of our personality that, although strongly influential, are not looked at much, if at all. All our behavior, however, hangs together; it is part of the mystery and wonder of the human condition. When we want to see ourselves whole, to see our actions as a language that leads us to a new self-understanding, we might well begin, the next time we are puzzled by some self-inflicted psychological reversal, by asking, "What are we getting out of this anyway?"

Chapter 6

AN EXAMPLE: THE MAN
WHO PUT THE WORLD
AT A DISTANCE

J AMES B. spoke with me recently and it was not easy for him. He said that he had suddenly discovered, in his mid-forties, that he had no friends, that nobody seemed to like him, and that his heart felt clammy from a loneliness he neither wanted nor understood. Here he was at a time when he theoretically should have been enjoying what he had achieved in life and yet he felt empty, unsatisfied, and inconsolably alone. James B. is not an unusual person; there are many people like him and most of them have no idea what to do about themselves. They dread the years of life that lie before them.

Actually, James B. made his life exactly the way it is. He is not a victim; he is the fashioner of his own situation, but he does not understand that it suits him to live so painfully. He is an extremely intelligent person with advanced degrees, who, until very recently, found himself always absorbed, somewhat like Ebenezer Scrooge, with the business at hand. I have seen a dozen different James B.'s in various roles, from parish priests to college professors to corporation executives and county judges. They are all the same. They substitute the use of their great intelligence for a more balanced development of themselves.

In their twenties and thirties they get away with it more easily. They are, after all, on the way up in their various endeavors in life, and they handle the emotional side of their existence by creating distance between themselves and other people, a cool, intellectual distance, a brook too broad for leaping. They keep everyone at a distance and pursue their own goals undistractedly. Many of them are very successful. Sooner or later, however, this adjustment catches up with them, especially when they look around in midlife and wonder what it all means.

Brilliant and frequently right on matters at issue, James B. has to be right all the time. He measures his relationships by the amount of argumentation he needs to employ in order to prevail. And argumentation is a style with him. No discussion is free of it, no matter how trivial, because he uses it to reassure himself of his own excellence and to keep people away at the same time. Relationship through constant dissent is his style — a closed mind making what he thought was a secure passage through life.

But now he has the job and money he wanted and the degree he worked so hard for and the presumed esteem of it all. He even has some kind of respect from other people who always knew him as a kind of argumentative fellow. But he doesn't have any love to speak of, and the people who could have been his friends got tired of arguing with him long ago.

Now he is lonely and afraid and life looks like a long antiseptic corridor. Even he is tired of fighting with people. It is quite late for James B. to begin restructuring his life, but it isn't *too* late. He can put himself back into the world of persons. It will not, however, be easy. The distance he must travel is exactly as far as he moved away from persons on his own years ago.

Chapter 7

GROWING UP: IT LOOKS
SO DIFFERENT FROM HERE

ONE OF THE MOST COMMON and yet most difficult of life's experiences requires us to re-examine our past and redefine it according to a more adult perspective. Because this is a hard thing to do we all put a filter, usually of rosy hue, on our memories. That is no news to any of us; our remembrance of things past is sweetened by the passage of time so that our worst gaffes and most embarrassing incidents are so well diluted that they leave no after-taste.

That is why nostalgia turns our hearts warm with longing for those good times, when we had real heroes, reliable faith, predictable weather, and the promise of true love. Those things seem so hard to get now, harder by far than the rationed items of any war time. That, of course, is why they look so appealing at a distance.

Because of the enchantment generated by that distance we find it painful to look deeply into the past lest we awaken memories and relationships that we would rather leave undisturbed. Yet this is a necessary feature of growing up, an essential task for anybody who wants to live honestly in the present.

Perhaps the greatest of these challenges is to redefine our own home life. We would all like to remember it as perfect, but a glorified memory is a distortion because no family is perfect and none ever will be. As a matter of fact, no healthy thing is perfect. When we forget this basic truth of life we get in trouble with both past and present.

Human beings thrive in environments that are healthy rather than perfect. If we suffer from a need to see the past as perfect, perhaps something unhealthy skulks there (just a little something anyway) that we do not really want to look at even though it is part of our history and a part of ourselves.

Probably the most sensitive area regarding our home life concerns our attitudes toward our parents. We don't like to say negative things about them no matter how human they are; lots of brawls are still triggered by hostile remarks about our ancestors. That we choose to attack on that level shows the significance and sensitivity we all share about our family trees. The worst insult in any culture is an assault on one's forebears.

But, when you are maturing, you can give up the idea that your parents are perfect without diminishing them in any way. You can admit their humanity without resenting them for it and without feeling shortchanged or disillusioned by life. Only the very fearful must hold on to a childhood view of their parents as great magical figures filling the sky and doing no wrong. These people never want to face the truth about themselves either, and life becomes a child's garden of verses, full of sunlight and statues, but not a place in which real people can live.

The time comes for all of us to put ourselves and our past into better perspective. It is important to be able to separate ourselves enough from the past to see it as it actually was, and thus better understand ourselves as we are. The need to see things realistically is not a call for debunking the past or blaming our parents for everything we manage to do wrong ourselves. We need not be cynically self-indulgent in the mode of Oscar Wilde's observation that "children begin by loving their parents; as they grow older they judge them; sometimes they forgive them."

Mature believers can see farther than that. They know that a more realistic view of their parents has a redemptive quality to it; they thereby free them from their own unreasonable demands that they be absolutely flawless. To see them more realistically may be to draw closer to them humanly, and to sense and possess what they have truly given to us so that we may hand it on to others.

Chapter 8

THE SYMPTOMS OF MATURITY

W E HAVE ALWAYS KNOWN, or at least reassured ourselves with the notion, that the path of true love is not always smooth. But, we might ask, isn't there a place where life levels off after the uphill struggles of growing up? Do not persons who do their best deserve at least a little quiet time to enjoy the fruits of growing up successfully? The answer to all these musings is negative.

If you find that your challenges balloon out when you think they should be diminishing; if you feel you are too tired to get up again but realize that life never lets you sit down for very long; if maturity, or the best you can make of it, is not exactly what you expected and life is even less fair than they warned you it would be; well, you are probably quite healthy and normal.

For these are the symptoms of maturity: not fewer problems but more of them, and more responsibility for solving them; not for a time of reflective contemplation after a race well run, but a steady grind marked by a few frenzied pit stops. Yes, and to make it all worse, mature persons have a deeper sensitivity to what is happening to them; they feel life's strain more than the immature.

So the difference between an adolescent and a mature adult is not that the adult has fewer problems. Mature people — and that, of course, has a relative kind of definition — are distinguished from immature people in the way they handle their problems. Mature people don't get out of trouble; they just get into more of it. However, when they are truly mature, they do cope with trouble more effectively.

The true measure of how adult we are, then, is our mode of reacting to challenges and difficulties; if our way of reacting to them causes us to taste them more painfully, it also enables us to handle them more constructively. Inspecting ourselves, we may be comforted by the signs of mature instincts that we did not realize we possess — encouraging signs that our attitudes are mature even when our woes multiply.

For example, mature adults minimize their use of denial or distortion in their understanding of themselves and their problems. They do not, in other words, fool themselves into thinking that there is nothing wrong when there is abundant evidence of a serious difficulty. One can cite a hatful of examples of immature distortion: the parents who steadfastly deny that their child has a problem even though the signs of it are there for all to see; the alcoholic who genially insists that he has control of his problem and that he is a lovable, good guy despite the harm he is doing to others; "cool" persons who deny their own feelings in order to preserve a fragile picture of their personality.

These immature stances present a false front toward life. How we look is often more important than how we really are. We can look good even when we are the least mature. We may yet go down in history as the culture that hid its true worries most stylishly; and if you don't think that clothes are a good defense against the blues, go out and buy something the next time you feel down. You won't be any more mature, but you will feel better — for a while.

Those who do not quite deny, but manage to distort, their problems give a slightly variant picture of the same personality dynamics. By whatever turn of phrase or turn of mind, it is always somebody else's fault — the boss, the neighbor, the wife, or conspirators of some kind. As they see it, the world teems with wickedness and they are innocents abroad, victims passive to the conspiring Fates. Oddly enough, the pose can also look good; some people get a lot of mileage out of being martyrs. And there are some who beg sympathy because they just never have had the breaks that other people get. We have always got it all wrong about them. They pass through life ungrown, not coping with their problems in an adult manner, not even feeling life's true rhythm or its authentic depth.

So if you have the feeling that things are getting worse for you instead of better, if your difficulties are growing more, rather than less, complicated, you should be properly grateful that you are honest and open enough to define yourself and your own world accurately. Maturity and the gauge of whether you possess it lie in the way you respond to the web of interwoven problems that by midlife seem to cover the sky itself. Maturity is the capacity to understand this and the willingness to pull ourselves together every day to take them all on again.

Chapter 9

BUT I DON'T FEEL LIKE IT...

WELL, MOST OF US do not feel like doing many of the things life flings in our paths during the course of a day. And it is not just old-fashioned wrong-headedness or an unredeemed Puritan ethic that motivates us to do things in spite of the way we feel. Americans have rediscovered their feelings — and they are responding to the messages they are receiving with varying degrees of maturity. Right now the measure of decision, commitment, being faithful, doing one's job, and half a dozen other things has come to be whether and how intensely a person feels about it.

Our feelings, of course, are good guides to action but only when we are willing and able to go beneath their surface to trace down and sort out the tangled roots of our various impulses. Emotions are not very dependable guides in the lives of persons who are unprepared or incapable of this kind of self-examination. Nevertheless, many people readily accept the first signals of their emotions; they make no effort to understand why the feeling is there in the first place.

This response, impulsive and undifferentiated, is all they need to set their course for the day or the week. In a way, this attitude is not very different from the response of the child who, when urged to do something, "doesn't feel like it"; a long process of learning must intervene before the child consciously alters that answer. When adults respond this way, it suggests that they have not passed beyond the child's level of self-comprehension and that this absorption with their own small world of feelings keeps them in exile from mature relationships with the larger world around them.

Allowing vague and ill-defined feelings to rule us is a far cry from the capacity of grown-up individuals to review their own emotions unselfconsciously as they make one decision or another. But self-examination is a difficult task, one that requires searching honesty and self-discipline as well as the ability to balance one's own inclinations against the rights and needs of other persons. Duty is not a dirty word for such persons; it is not dysfunctional to tackle distasteful chores. Adults are not strangers to faint-heartedness in times of challenge or queasiness at the prospect of fulfilling a difficult obligation, but they do not give up when they head into the contrary winds of their own emotions.

The mature are not afraid to integrate clashing feelings and to let their own desires take second place in the order of action. The mature, perhaps a dozen or more times a day, do things that in some way or other they do not feel like doing. That is to say, they are grown-up rather than hung-up on making the universe spin around their own personalities.

In the Bible we read that Christ himself was not surprised to discover and deal with reluctant feelings at various occasions. You can sense his drawing himself together in the face of obstacles, not in some superhuman manner, with the unflinching plastic control that some evangelists attribute to him, but with the realization of crosscurrents within himself. He had to deal with many feelings — from sadness at the death of Lazarus to desolation in the Garden of Gethsemane.

Christ was obviously aware of the many levels of his human emotions, but he had a sense of their interrelationship and of the values that guided him. A little death goes into every reordering of our own feelings at those times when, if it were left totally up to us, we might say the hell with it. But those kinds of deaths of self give life to the full-bodied maturity of those who are not afraid of facing a life filled with things they do not feel like doing.

Chapter 10

BEGINNING AGAIN

N EW BEGINNINGS ABOUND in the many different areas of our lives. We must take up the frustrating little tasks that go along with the pursuit of the greatest ideals. Indeed, being human seems at times to be nothing other than beginnings. Families, in nomadic North America, must begin again the search for friends in a succession of new neighborhoods. With promotions or job changes, people face the renewed challenge of proving themselves with yet another group of colleagues. The head of the house, in face of a thousand drudgeries, must carry on in getting together the tax and the mortgage money, or in finding the cash to educate the children. Parents let their children begin their own lives and find that they themselves must begin a new phase. And wise persons, who think they have heard of almost all of life's problems, discover that there is always something new, something unexpected in its challenge to their response.

We are all painting the George Washington Bridge. The accomplishment of finishing merely brings us to the task of starting all over again, always swaying above buzzing traffic and bitter waters.

Even love is filled with new beginnings and repeated tests of faithfulness. These come in a hundred ways — after doubts and misunderstandings, in-law trouble and illnesses. Even those people who know and love each other very deeply are at times surprised by sudden flashes of insight that seem to be just the beginning of a new understanding of each other.

Our relationships turn corners in time, and love that is truly responsible must measure up to an endless set of challenges. Real love never gets to rest on its oars in life; it is always active, always seeking a fresh understanding of things, or it isn't love at all. Real lovers must keep working at it, and there is always something new about what they find in life and in each other.

But how hard it is really to make all things new in a relationship that is under stress. How hard to forgive each other for the fresh, often unconscious hurts we can exchange every day. Sometimes it seems easier to nurse old grudges than to face the new beginnings that forgiveness urges on us.

It is hard always to begin again, whether at trying to be better, or more loving, or to do our work with greater integrity. Easier by far to let the lines of compromise be drawn bold across life and to insulate ourselves behind them. Was there ever an age where not beginning difficult things, never getting around to it, putting it off, or never ending something was more exalted?

It is not surprising that we might yearn for what we now think were the good old days — the days before satellites, computers, the Space/Information Age trumping its own accomplishments before we grasp them, the splendid quiet days before the world turned topsy-turvy on us. Spiritual persons ask how many times they must begin again, or how many times they must be ready to let others begin again in relationship to them. Seventy times seven is not enough to count the believers' challenges to start fresh, to be born again, not sinless but not cynical either.

That is, in fact, the real miracle of religious faith. It is set in the Testament of the New, ordered to the fresh possibilities rather than the old mistakes of life. It proclaims that availability of the Spirit who would breathe on the earth and make it a New Creation. We are never irrevocably lost or trapped by the sins of our youth. Religious faith is necessarily a vehicle of hope that reassures us that we can rise from our own daily baths, that we can be renewed as persons in the Spirit. Both our redemption and our maturity are achieved precisely in the shifting human condition where with every dawn we make a fresh start on the many tasks of being human.

The spiritual life is not a die-straight road into the future. It is more like a maze, laden with wrong turns and dead ends, with surprises and difficulties. We make our way through. That is why there is more joy over the one sheep found than the ninety-nine who never strayed. We are that sheep we read about in the Bible. Finding ourselves and starting out again is the daily work of the spiritual life.

The difficulties of the contemporary world and trials of personal life seem enough to discourage the strongest of us. The temptations to sue for a private peace with the ever-changing world are many and great. Believers know that there is no end to their need to begin again, but they also know that God's promises are the guarantee that they always can begin again. That is what the resurrected life of the Spirit looks like. Nothing fancy, really. Many would call it homely. That is why it fits us so well. And that is the way we give light and life to a dark and dispirited world.

Chapter 11

"DO NOT GO GENTLE..."

"**D**O NOT GO GENTLE into that good night." So, we are often reminded, wrote Dylan Thomas, the Welsh poet. Rage, he urged, rage against the dying of the light. The trouble is that we live in an age in which people have increasingly justified going quite gently and quite passively into more than the good night of death. We have gone a long way in rationalizing our way out of ever having to face and work through pain, anxiety, or even an occasional sleepless night. Better by far to blame others, and sedate away our pain, a prescription that lets us lie down in limbo for a while. No raging here; just a search for quiet and for at least a few moments when life doesn't hurt quite so much. Well, who can blame modern people, harried, criticized, told that things were never worse, from taking whatever excuse or relief they can find?

The next time you are tempted to join the passive minority ask yourself whether it might not be good to meet the pain or loneliness head on for a change. This is not an invitation to masochism. Perhaps pain can be conquered only by taking it on as any enemy who must be faced down with quarter neither given nor requested. We have more resources than we usually think; we may never discover them, and therefore never discover ourselves fully, if we do not enter the pain and suffering that test our depths and test them true. There is a place in life for the experience of pain, not for its own sake, but because it burns the dross off us in a way that nothing else can.

If we never fight the battle of suffering out in the open, with full consciousness of what it is all about, we may miss something that is essential to being fully grown. We will miss the full measure of friendship that takes on its meaning, not in the passed cups of celebration, but in sharing the chalice of anguish; we will never know real love because in trying to perpetuate romance we will not face the fierce and lonely moments when lovers look like strangers to each other; we will not know the full face of life because we have been afraid to look steadily into the eyes of death.

Persons estranged from pain resemble children overmedicated against the infant diseases so that they never build up a strong inner immunity against them; those who never learn to live with pain only make themselves more vulnerable to it. I am not defending the large measure of unnecessary suffering that is found everywhere in life. No one in his right mind would do anything but attempt to lessen this in all its forms. I refer to the inevitable sufferings of life, the pains that shape our existence, the pains that must be faced because they cannot be fended off. We who name the birds and the beasts must put the right name on our agonies if we are to do battle with and down them.

"We are healed of a suffering," Marcel Proust wrote, "only by experiencing it to the full." Redemption lies, then, in sifting our real from our fancied problems and in dealing with both of them realistically. Some people cover their real problems with imaginary problems to such an extent that they never can tell the symptom from the real suffering. They have terrible headaches in place of working through the difficulties of a tangled personal relationship; in fact the headaches excuse them from even understanding where the real problem lies. People are ordinarily afraid that they will miss the meaning of life if they miss one of its possible pleasures; they run a far greater risk of missing its meaning when they shy away from its sufferings.

The example of Jesus is powerful to believers and non-believers alike. Christ dreaded but actively accepted the pain that was inseparable from his role as the redeeming servant of the world. He knew what people would do to him and neither looked away from the suffering itself nor from understanding the complex motives of his persecutors. He faced and conquered suffering and death; he did not surrender to them. That is resurrection.

Our involvement in the continuing mystery of redemption bids us to deal with our own personal pains in a similar fashion. This is not the stoic refusal to admit that pain can lay a hand on us. It is rather our own active entrance into our sufferings, our standing up against them or grappling toe to toe with them while the light lasts; that is the way of resurrection because that is the true way of life.

The Spirit comes to us when we remember the worth, as the apostle Paul put it, of fighting the good fight and of not wasting our blows on the empty air. Perhaps he meant that his refusal to go gently into the night of suffering was a way of keeping faith with himself and his true identity as a man and as an apostle. So rage a little against the real suffering in your life; face it down and find resurrection.

Chapter 12

OUR DEFENSE TEAM

WE NEED NOT BE DEFENSIVE about using psychological defenses. Everybody uses psychological defenses. Even the healthiest person finds them functional at times; little white lies, exaggerations, making ourselves sound better motivated than we are: These are but a few of the maneuvers that the best of human beings recognize as their own. Indeed, such defenses reveal all of us in the less than perfect, but quite normal, condition that is human. It is only when the use of defenses becomes the main manner in which we relate to life that we may be described as not functioning well.

Why do average persons turn to some form of defensive response in the course of everyday life? Ordinarily this occurs at a moment when we are caught off guard, or unprepared for a novel experience, or when we have not fully come to terms with some aspect of our personality. We erect defenses around areas that we are not prepared to share fully with other people, even in such questions as our political affiliation, our interest in sports or the arts, or just how much we get paid.

We all want to appear intelligent, assured, and in control of ourselves and our lives. When we are suddenly challenged in some set of circumstances, a little defensiveness is quite helpful in smoothing over the small gaps of anxiety that then pop open. So we say something we really do not mean, or assert a claim that is not entirely invalid, or change the subject to something that takes the heat off us.

Modern American males are, for example, sometimes uneasy if they fail to exhibit a thoroughgoing interest in and knowledge about athletics. A little defensiveness, a measure of contrived enthusiasm, and they pass muster with the rest of the boys about the current sports scene. Or, working it the other way around, they may feel embarrassed by their interest in poetry or the opera but never admit it to their friends to avoid giving the impression that they take culture seriously. So, too, there are areas that are nobody else's business, such as the size of one's paycheck. A little backing and filling, a grumble about taxes, and a quick change of subject may be employed instead of a straightforward refusal to answer the question.

We sometimes employ relatively harmless defenses to make ourselves look better than we know, in our heart of hearts, we really are. There is, for example, the slow transformation of the good story we have been telling for years. At first it was something we had heard about; gradually, in the retelling, we eliminate the middle man and tell it as if we had been present; in the final version, we have simplified it to the point that we are no longer the observant reporter but the main character. We can get pretty good at this, so good, in fact, that after a period of time we really believe the story ourselves and would raise our hand and swear to it as an eyewitness in court.

All these examples have something in common with all defense mechanisms, even those that are signs of deeper personal problems. Basically, each defense employs an aspect of denial or disguise of the truth. They all varnish reality a little for the same purpose — to give a better picture of the personality. We employ them, in milder situations, for exactly the same reason that more disturbed people do — to hold ourselves together and even to enhance ourselves in moments of uneasiness. We get defensive, in other words, whenever our familiar picture of ourselves is under threat because some of our actions or feelings contradict or do not really fit in with this self-portrait we have hung, softly lit, in our imaginations for a long time.

Defenses arise when inconsistencies begin to show through at some level of our consciousness. These inconsistencies make us anxious and the defenses have the very functional effect of toning down that anxiety. We bridge our normal inconsistencies with defensive statements or behavior because it is much easier to do this than it is to reexamine and possibly change the picture we have of ourselves. We use defenses because, in the words of Saul Bellow, "the unexamined life may not be worth living but the examined life is driving me crazy."

For example, the persons who think of themselves as always in control of their feelings are quite threatened by a sudden impulse of anger. It just doesn't fit the way they identify themselves. The

strong feeling challenges their supposedly secure self-knowledge.
But the anger is there bubbling away ominously and something has
to be done about it. When we are surprised by such a contradictory
feeling, our first impulse is to deny it, precisely because of its incon-
sistency with our idea of ourselves. "No, I'm not angry!" we will
say, erecting a first line of defense against this intrusive feeling.

The strange thing, of course, is that we may say this in such a
clearly defensive tone of voice that we actually reveal our anger
to everybody anyhow. But that is not the point here; the defenses
serve us, our own inner world, our cherished picture of ourselves.
We deny anger in order to put it out of the way. This is obviously
not a very good long-term strategy but it may be very effective for
the moment. This is exactly where defenses are put to good use
by healthy persons. They give us time to think, they remove the
pressure of the instant, and they may make it possible for us to
take a fresh look at ourselves once the initial sense of threat has
tapered off a bit.

The popular ideal we have of being completely open and
defenseless in all our relationships is unrealistic even for the
soundest of human beings. Because we are not perfect, because
self-discovery is an ongoing process, and because defenses are not
always terribly bad things, we should not be too disappointed to
find vestiges of defensive behavior in our lives. We should be surprised if they were *not* there as we would if we did not find moss
on trees or dew on grass.

We may quite gradually be able to eliminate most of it, but we
should not necessarily feel that they are unhealthy because they
cannot do this all at once or completely at any time. In fact, some
people who demand an instant and total openness from others may
be less healthy than individuals who are less than ready to bare
their innermost secrets with complete candor.

Growth in openness occurs through time in the only way that
any growth process takes place. Some form of defense is probably
necessary for us average wayfarers struggling to understand ourselves fully enough to be more completely open to our fellows. We
must respect this truth, both in ourselves and in our friends, and
not rudely tear down, from the outside, defensive structures that
can only be given up, in the long run, from within.

Chapter 13

SOMETIMES IT'S BETTER
TO LEAVE YOUR MASK ON

S OMETIMES IT'S BETTER to leave your mask on even though it is the fashion to take it off at midnight or once Halloween has safely passed. As a matter of fact, one of the most overworked clichés in the age of personalism runs pretty much the same. People are constantly being accused of wearing masks, of hiding their true selves behind them; the ethos of a confessional age says we are to remove these masks or have them stripped away in the name of more fulfilling relationships. Contemporary salvation comes through self-exposure and there is, of course, something to be said for a right understanding of this. There are times, however, when it is not a bad idea to keep our masks on, times when we should respect others enough to let them keep theirs on too if they wish.

Although it is good that we have grown to value an honest exchange of feelings, some individuals have made this an intense and humorless personal crusade. They permit no quiver of feeling, no matter how insignificant, to go unexpressed. It is out in the open with everything here and now without delay and without even a bow in the direction of good manners. In the lexicon of the unmaskers, such an attitude is very "real," very "gutsy," very "now." Take off your mask and join the party; let everybody know what you really feel about them and everything else. This usually consists in telling others how you dislike yourself or your victimizing parents, how you don't take anything, how you get the other before the other gets you.

Any real sensitivity to human relationships, however, dictates that there are times when we should keep masks and our feelings firmly in place. The very fact that we experience and recognize certain feelings does not mean that we must express them. Our emotions are not churning around just waiting to be siphoned out publicly in a raw and unprocessed state. That, however, is what some people want when they drop their masks and urge you to do the same. Life is all feeling, without a forgiving smile for one's foibles. Few understand that feeling, important as it is, is only a part of human life.

We live in an age in which nobody tells you what they think. They only want us to know how they feel. We don't have to play life with a poker face to recognize the wisdom of moderating our emotional responses. If we let go with some primal burst every time we are frustrated, crossed by another, or hurt by something in life, we will soon self-destruct. If we want a response to our feelings now and cannot tolerate any delay, we will go through life like babies who respond only to their impulses. Sometimes it is hard work to keep ourselves together, difficult indeed to maintain the mask of control when we want to rip it off and sail it away like a frisbee.

So, maintaining ourselves is important for our own stability and growth; it is also important for others. We cannot let our feelings fly when there are those around us who either cannot handle such onslaughts very well or who would be deeply offended by our determined honesty. We must, in other words, keep a mask on our feelings whenever we would otherwise make ourselves a burden to others. And that covers a wide variety of situations, from remaining calm in the face of disaster to keeping our courage up so that others won't lose theirs. These are the foundations of good manners, the rituals by which we respect and make life with each other possible.

The masks we preserve in these situations are not phony cover-ups for our real selves; sometimes they are the better side of ourselves, the side that is revealed only when the pressure is on and the stakes are high. It is clear, however, that persons who let themselves go emotionally are living in response only to their own feelings and that they are incapable of taking the feelings of others into account. Despite the claims of the passionate unmaskers, revealing all your feelings all the time is not adult but childish. And besides, some of us look better with masks on anyway.

Chapter 14

LIVING BY DEFENSES:
ONE-LINERS INSTEAD OF LIFE

"I DIDN'T KNOW you were so sensitive." People usually say that to us after they have made some remark that hurts us deeply. It is odd that they should be surprised to discover that, after they set out to hurt us, they really have caused us pain. Sometimes people play a dangerous game with their jests, skating a hazardous pattern across the thin ice of our self-esteem, hoping, with the excitement of a young boy on a winter pond, to get away with it.

Others play the game from a distance, using greater subtlety and style. Characters on sit-coms converse almost exclusively in put-down language. The phenomenon of persons relating through razor-edged one-liners is so universal that it bears closer inspection.

The put-down is a substitute for richer and better things, a defensive mask to hide features shrivelled by loneliness, a way of staying loose and keeping people from getting too close. The very words "put-down" bear seeds of malice in them; they are a sort of giveaway signal that this is not a game for good-natured friends as much as a stylized hostility that just looks as though it doesn't hurt.

Often and oddly enough, the fast remarks drain off bad feelings that have little, if anything, to do with the person we put down. Our cleverness celebrates ourselves and some unresolved aspect of our own personality. The whole idea is to go one up by putting the other guy down. A strange self-serving dynamic is at work here through which we express our own discomfort while keeping others at a distance. People who relate this way develop a sixth sense for discovering the most vulnerable area of the other. It is not exactly a fair way to fight; this offense as defense gets others where it hurts them badly.

Everybody knows persons who have learned "to keep others in their place" with their verbal anti-personnel weapons. These individuals say that they don't mean to hurt you but do it just the same. It is, in the long run, a bad business, giving the attackers the freedom from others they want for the moment but also leaving them isolated. This defense really works. It keeps people away from us. A sharp tongue is not much of a companion for a desperate old age. Maybe we ought to think of that the next time we are tempted to slaughter some innocent.

And how do you like the guys who are the first to transmit some bad news to you? They try to strike a sympathetic note, something like a murderer whistling while he goes for your jugular vein. Writers are familiar with the alleged friend who alerts them to a terrible review that is about to appear. "What did you ever do to so and so" they ask, "that she would criticize you like this?" Variants on this first-in-line-to-zing-you are found in all walks of life. Friends they may claim to be but friends they are not, to themselves or others.

There are, however, things we can learn in the hand-to-hand combat that catches us just where we are weakest; a whole profile emerges from the tender reference points of our psyche. In other words, a little more courage to look at what we feel touchiest about may help us to know ourselves better. Often, the things we look away from are the very ones that betray us in life, those problem areas we could have approached and done something about if we had been a little less sensitive and a little more willing to learn.

Probably the most important thing we can learn from these situations is the power we ourselves have to hurt others, especially in close-range relationships with our family and with those we love. Imitating sit-com dialogue is not much of a way to live; it is neither good psychology nor good philosophy. It certainly is not living by faith. We should resolve to become more conscious of the moments when we can really damage others and try to avoid these easy chances. We may hurt less, but everybody will be enjoying it more.

Chapter 15

PERFECTIONISM

THE DESIRE to do things perfectly has always seemed praise-worthy enough, so praiseworthy, indeed, that some people are surprised to discover that perfectionism has a long and fabled history as a psychological defense. In principle, perfectionism works like the rest of the defenses; when something slips into the edge of our awareness that doesn't fit the picture we have of ourselves we automatically set up a barrier of denial or disguise against it in order to maintain our good opinion of ourselves. Defenses turn away, at least temporarily, the anxiety we would feel if we took a long hard look at what is really going on inside ourselves.

So it is with perfectionism. When we are unconsciously uneasy about doing something, even when it is an important thing to get done, we invoke the mechanism of perfectionism. We hold on to whatever it is — the book we are writing, the decision we are supposed to make, the opinion we are asked to form — telling our-selves and others that we haven't got it quite right yet, that it needs a few added touches, that the times aren't right, or that we need more information.

However we describe it, we are playing the perfectionism game, the time-buying device that protects us from the possibility of con-flict of criticism. Persons caught up in the perfectionism routine never get anything finished because they never get anything quite right; it is actually easier on them to postpone things than to take the risk of making some kind of mistake or allowing the world to see that they are fallible after all. A colleague in graduate school worked for years on a plan for a doctoral thesis, seeking a holy grail kind of perfection in his research that would make it unique and immune from criticism. The fear of not covering every possi-bility, the anxiety over taking any risk at all paralyzed him. The years wasted away and the thesis was never written. He lost in a certain way, but in the inner world of his own personality he kept on winning. He used the defense of perfectionism with the skill of a field marshal. He never had to take a chance and he never was criticized, but he missed the doctorate and the chance to grow at the same time.

The examples of perfectionism in action are not hard to find. In what we used to term religious scrupulosity, for example, persons are so preoccupied with saying their prayers right that they never get them finished. Their religious life is confined to a very small area of obsessive concern, and they never look beyond this. There is something dissociative about this kind of defense, a breaking off of some thought or action from the feeling that should go with it.

Through perfectionism, like stepping on all the cracks in the sidewalk or repeating some prayers endlessly, persons hold back a tide of worry that would otherwise engulf them. That is why these devices, simple though they may seem, are of such significance to those who use them. These people are trying to solve their problem through these little rituals, holding the hounds of life at bay by snapping the frayed whip of this defense. When people get tangled in this defense, they need psychological help.

Perfectionism, however, is also found among people who seem to have something of value to contribute to the world. They hold back out of fear, waiting for fairer weather, or until added years or some other event makes it safe for them to write their book, make their decision, or even get married. They want to delay until they are able to do it perfectly, and that, of course, is a very long and self-defeating interval disguised as virtue.

Fear is the enemy of most of our growth, and perfectionism is not an easy defense for the fearful to put aside. A first step, however, is the realization that the defense is very crippling and, in the long run, one that shuts persons out from life and from other people. It also keeps them from ever tapping their own resources fully and freely or from the liberating discovery that the spiritual life — indeed, life in general — is designed for imperfect people. And that is a discovery that no fear should make us postpone, for now is the acceptable time, now is the time of salvation.

Chapter 16

FIRST, DO NO HARM

L IFE RUNS, if it runs at all, on the energy we generate through believing in and loving each other. When the world runs out of that, it will have no power supply left at all, no matter how many new caverns of oil are discovered under the tundra or how much energy is beamed down from the stars. When our supply of trust is exhausted, the world will be chilled for good, and the chiaroscuro night will last forever. We have a terrible power to plunge our fellow humans into darkness by suspending or holding back our belief in them. Unfortunately, we sometimes do that just at the wrong moment, just at the moment, in fact, when others are in great need of the support that comes from our confidence in them. Of all the ways there are not to be helpful, suspension of trust is near the head of the list.

We say, however, that it is hard to keep hoping in other people, even in those who are closest to us in our family or circle of friends. We hedge on hope and trust because we accumulate so many scars in giving it out to other people who then blow the whole thing like gamblers with the family fortune and disappoint us bitterly. So we get over the idea of being cheerfully optimistic about our children or our friends and their good intentions and brave promises.

We have seen, we say, too many compromises made in the course of life to believe unqualifiedly in other people. We hold back, muttering to ourselves, "Well...," "Maybe...," "You'll never make it," or something else that tells the truth about our feelings toward the other. And that feeling, that strong current rolling across our psyche, is what we communicate to others, no matter what we say in words to them.

If there is one thing that takes the wind out of persons, it is the sudden and uneasy realization that their friend or brother does not really trust them, that they are on the outside after all, that they are looked on as those who might do the wrong thing rather than those trying to do the right thing. That is a crushing blow especially for growing persons who so much need older persons to believe in them and let them work out some decision or solve some problem in their own way.

For grown-ups it is discouraging to discover that friends they rely on are a little skeptical about their trustworthiness after all. Take the edge off your belief in others and you may do just the thing that guarantees they will make a mess of something. When we feel that others do not trust us fully, we find it hard to keep on trusting ourselves.

There is no doubt that we can be foolish in giving support to other people when we do not know much about what they are doing, or when we are not close enough to them to be real about it. There are all kinds of reasons for staying at a distance, or for warning people about their possible mistakes. That is easy to do because it doesn't cost anything and it is the most cautious hand to play in human relations. We won't make many mistakes if we follow that course; we won't have many friends either. Instead, our lives will be filled with people we are afraid of or afraid for. This may be a defensively secure way to live but it is also an unhappy one.

Spiritual men and women move from feeling responsible *for* other people to feeling responsible *to* other people. There is a big difference, as the wise and the loving can tell you. But sticking with other people even as we grant them the freedom to make what they will of their own decisions and their own lives is one of the hardest lessons to learn. Not even husbands and wives are responsible for each other; their love stays alive when they are able to be responsible to each other, and that takes large stringless investments of belief.

Never have we been so tempted to give up on each other as we are in our day, to save ourselves and to salvage what we can of the possible happiness in our own lives. Never have we needed more the generous kind of support that makes the believer's commitment to other people the most creative and confronting development in the history of the world. The latter needs us to believe and to trust, not as cynical schoolmasters ready to punish the failures we can already foresee, but as persons who live by and give life through their everyday reactions. And it might be a good idea to begin with each other today — or at least to resolve not to give up on each other today.

Chapter 17

RESCUE FANTASIES:
DO-GOODERS' DELIGHTS

THERE ARE PEOPLE — some of them may be bearing down on you at this very moment — who want to save you from yourself by solving your problems for you. Now, that is all very well, you say, but where were they when I needed them, like last week when I was short of cash or last month when my in-laws came for a visit?

We might as well be clear about these saviors right from the start. They do not respond to your need for help; they respond to their need to help you.

It is quite possible — in fact, very likely — that your needs and their needs to not coincide. These proverbial helpers experience what psychiatry describes as "rescue fantasies." They live according to an imaginative picture of themselves charging off to snatch someone from an impending disaster. And the world is full of them.

People who live by these heroic visions of themselves are not necessarily aware of their fantasy. It is so much a part of their make-up that they seldom reflect on it or look very deeply into themselves for its roots. Quite often they do a lot of good — and there is no sense in knocking good, even if it sometimes comes about in strange ways.

Many individuals motivated by rescue fantasies cannot relate to people unless the people are in trouble; that is, they can give themselves to others only when the others are in some demonstrable need. And, instead of recognizing their own need to "rescue" others, they often imagine that others are helpless and they rush to them with the bright light of "I'll save you" in their eyes.

There are times when we should give all the help and support to others that we can; but there are other times when it is best that we leave them alone. Ultimately, we must face up to and deal with our own problems by ourselves. Many times overhelpful persons spreading rescue nets beneath our lives deny us the chance to do something that, unless we do it for ourselves, will not save us anyway.

When we are in trouble, or even in deep sorrow, we need our friends around; they are the best friends, however, when they make themselves present but do not take our lives or our troubles out of our own hands. Our best friends, after all, are friends precisely because they know how to give themselves to us; that is what makes them different from the eager do-gooders dominated by rescue fantasies.

The latter take us over for themselves. They are the main characters in their wispy little visions of helping others. Their fantasies pull them like magnets from warm beds, quiet vacations, and pleasant home lives to rush to our side. But it is always the rescuer at our side who is really in the limelight, the person who really cannot live a normal and uninterrupted life and who contrives quite successfully not to. In fact, so good are they that you do not have a problem until they arrive at your side. It may, in the long run, be hard to tell whether the emergency attracts the rescue fancier or the rescue fancier attracts the emergency.

We may need an organization, Helpers' Anonymous, to deal with do-gooders. When members experience the overpowering urge to help somebody else, they call up another member for support until the urge passes.

In any case, those who live by rushing off to solve other people's problems quite often do more harm than good. They have not yet learned that there are some things nobody can do much about, some emotions just too hot to touch, some wounds too tender to probe. At the same time, they may be leaving their own lives in a relatively constant state of emergency, letting their own relationships deteriorate while they are busy trying to patch up those of others.

The worst danger, then, is for those who live by these fantasies. They take them out of the real world, enable them to escape their more intimate responsibilities, and perpetuate the fiction that they are helping when they are actually only meddling. The next time you are tempted to think you are the only one who can save the world, or even your next door neighbor, think it over again. The mental health you save may be your own.

Chapter 18

WHAT DO YOU DO
WHEN NOTHING CAN BE DONE?

THERE IS EXCITEMENT in a demanding and clearly defined challenge; healthy people sometimes feel exhilaration in solving
problems and overcoming obstacles in order to achieve some
greater good. Often, the best in us comes out when we see an
attractive goal and feel the tension of summoning up our inven-
tory of strengths in order to reach it. More than the best of us is
needed, however, when, despite our desire and willingness to do
almost anything, situations arise that render us helpless.

What do we do when there is nothing we can do, nothing defi-
nite anyway, to make ourselves feel that at least we have tried our
best or done our damnedest?

Such moments come into every life at those times when there is
just no sure guide about what can be done to make things better.
We feel at a loss then, thrown back on the resources of our spirit,
left to rediscover the kind of hope we need to make our way in
the dark. It happens to parents, for example who have done everything they can for their children; there comes a time when parents
must allow their children to make their own decisions about their
directions and ideals in life. It can be hard to let go of a young man
or woman, especially when he or she still seems hardly more than
a child.

Should one let them go into the unsmiling world when they seem
all too vulnerable to the ways in which the world can hurt them?
There is, in fact, nothing to do but let them go; we cannot live,
grow, or, as the old saying goes, cry for them. But still it is difficult
for us to accept this fact; it is hard for us to know when we cannot
do anything more than what we have already done.

This trying problem comes up in many other situations. It may
happen that we have friends — a married couple for example —

who are out of touch with each other, their communication shattered, their bitterness against each other sharply honed. We want
to help but there is nothing anyone can do when their wounds are
too tender to touch. Occasionally, well-meaning friends display an
ironic talent for hurting when they really mean to heal. It is difficult, indeed, to learn the art of being a friend who knows how
to be there without intruding. Such persons know just what to do
when there is nothing to be done.

Or suppose, as so often happens, the situation is completely out
of our hands; there is nothing we could do even if we wanted
to. For example, there are heart-rending moments of waiting in
hospital corridors and doctors' offices while somebody we love
is beyond our words or our touch; they exist for the moment in
that hazy atmosphere of unnecessary sickness or uncertain diagnosis that we cannot enter no matter how much we ache to do so.
There are times when all we can do is wait with those we love,
wait for the words we are afraid to hear, or for the decisions we
wish did not have to be made.

At such times we are laid bare as persons and our interior sub-
stance or lack of it becomes plain in the charged space where all
distractions fail, when we must face the unknown — with someone
we love — as best we can. In these moments we must tame our
restlessness and let our pride die because there is absolutely nothing we can do; we can only be with the other as fully as we can.
And that is as hard as anything in life.

It means learning that we do not always have to be doing something in order to love and help others. In fact, it means that we
must learn to make ourselves present to another just as we are,
putting away our own wishes and fighting off self-pity. This is precisely the time when our loved ones need us; not what we can do or
say, but just us, as we are, to be with them through the long hours
when it takes extreme effort to keep our courage from collapsing
with the next deep breath.

This is the time we learn to pray again, when we dig deep inside
ourselves for the sincerity we may have mislaid. This is the moment
of truth — when we learn whether we have guts, or character, or
if we have ever learned anything about love. We only appear to be
doing nothing. We are really doing the most important thing of all.

Chapter 19

WHAT TO DO WHEN YOU'RE FEELING DOWN

P ROBABLY NO SUBJECT has inspired more advice than that malady, more common than the common cold itself, that has many names and no name at all. I mean, of course, that frayed stage curtain that falls unexpectedly and rudely across our day to leave us without enthusiasm, energy, or even much hope. Call it the blues or the blahs; everybody knows what this experience is like, but few of us have learned to cope with it successfully.

We usually wait for it to pass, and sooner or later it does; in the meantime we go through the motions of life as best we can. It is like being caught in an airport because of a fog that we can neither pray nor propel away; we just wait in the uncomfortable chairs, a restless and steamy crowd of fellow travelers milling about us, until the overcast lifts away by itself.

But is that all we can do? Not according to those who love to give advice — be it philosophical ("Into each life some rain must fall") or physiological ("work out at a fitness club"). Some of us have tried all of these solutions and ended up wiser, if not less melancholic, for all our exertions. We never feel so good as at the moment when our mood or depression begins to dissipate. "How," we ask ourselves, "did I get over this one?" — thinking if only we could remember this evaporating combination we might apply it earlier the next time we free fall into the dumps. But the reasons why we emerge from the blackness are as hard to identify as the reasons we sink into it. What can we do?

There are several solutions which we can quickly put aside. These include drinking, daydreaming, and drug taking. These are popular ways of escaping from the very real pain of being down. However, their distracting or mollifying effects on us are usually tragically temporary, and when their magic is over we are more depressed than ever — and no closer to understanding why. There is nothing easier to talk oneself into than a couple of quick ones to burn away the day's accumulated dross from the soul. Medication has become an automatic response in the Prozac Nation, but drugs need a skilled physician's monitoring if they are to be truly beneficial.

If left to our own resources we might remember that ups and downs are rather normal and they do not generally require drastic medicines or overkill responses. There is something to be said for the Far Eastern method of letting ourselves swim with the tide of life even when it is running against us. Thrashing about blindly may cost us more energy and generate more frustration than it is really worth. Most people have cyclic moods, and they should not get too upset when they occur. It does not mean that they have bipolar illness and need lithium.

For average persons, a few moments of self-reflection may help them to understand why their emotions have suddenly taken a nose dive. The trouble, of course, is that when we do not feel very well we do not feel like inspecting our emotions either. That is one of the reasons that a little snag in our day can have such a powerfully depressing effect on us.

Suddenly, overcast emotional weather comes from a rapidly forming front of small hurts or disappointments — a big storm touched off by a lot of little lows in our everyday life. For example, upon rising, a man may feel fairly fit and ready to work energetically all day. At breakfast, however, his wife brings up something that takes the air out of him — such as telling him that he is beginning to put on weight, or getting gray hair, or that there is some evidence that their oldest son is smoking pot, or that her mother is arriving for a month's visit that very afternoon. In short, the sweetmeats saved from the night before. In varying ways, these little announcements can depress anybody, deflating and turning what promised to be a good day into a long journey into night. Let us take a closer look.

Sudden reminders of our mortality are not so startling; we can read the calendar as well as anybody else. It is just that a reminder of that sort usually comes at the wrong moment — it is often out of tune with our general mood and is the kind of information we do not like to think about anyway. This is typical of the small events, so tiny that we are not aware of their impact at the time, that get into our bloodstream with a subtle but sure effect on our general well-being. These are small blows (little murders, if you will) so glancing that we hardly admit them into our consciousness — hardly, in other words, give a name to them when they occur. Their effect is nonetheless telling, in part because the nature of these problems is such that we do not like to admit, even to ourselves, that such things bother us.

But they nibble at us, these psychological viruses of the human condition, sapping our strength all day long. To handle these situations adequately we must trace the path of our depression back to the incident that set it off. This takes time and honesty. A sense of humor beats Prozac. Otherwise we might be appalled at the size or character of the event that laid us low. A good laugh, as we recognize our human frailty, is very therapeutic.

Learning that someone near and dear to you may have a serious problem is a much more obvious source of depression — especially if we get the information at an awkward time and cannot do anything about it. There is a strange economy in the business of breaking bad news; we frequently do it at the worst possible time for the person to whom we communicate it, e.g., just as the other is going to work, or off on a trip, or after a long day.

We might pause at such a time and think about what we can do and when we can effectively do it. Dealing with the problem realistically, even if it means delaying our response until a better time, eliminates much of the depression that would otherwise arise. This course demands a little time and reflection, but it is better than a day of agonized and indecisive worry; although it is not a perfect solution, given the human condition, it is about as good as they come.

Well, how about the mother-in-law coming? It could be the husband's mother just as easily. Just think of Franklin D. Roosevelt slipping that in at the last moment to Eleanor. That kind of news, slipped in when there is no time to discuss it, may be upsetting, but it also points to another problem that deserves our attention. If the communication between a husband and wife is so edgy that these unexpected announcements are always being made without previous warnings or intelligence reports, the marriage relationship itself needs to be examined.

A man and woman who are gradually drifting out of phase with each other master little techniques that, like warning salvos from a visiting fleet, upset and intimidate each other. Husbands and wives get to be very good at such war games, knowing from their years together the exact location of each other's soft spots. Such a marriage slowly turns into a kind of hell as the couple's communication gradually disintegrates. A man cannot successfully focus on the little depressions in this kind of relationship; either he decides to get much deeper into the causes of this hostility or he will not have much of a marriage left and may end up communicating more clearly to his local bartender than to his wife.

As a matter of fact, if you really want to get to the bottom of your bad moods, try listening to the way you talk about your life and hard times to others, whoever they are. With some careful listening you may catch many hints of what you are really like as a person. You may even be able to siphon off the self-pity that so easily becomes a part of complaining. You will get a better picture of yourself and your own role in your depressions than you could get from a bookful of self-help philosophy. And if you listen to yourself long enough you may begin to smile, and then to laugh a little at the inconsistencies of your own position. Before you know it, you will feel much better. And those closest to you will feel better, too.

Chapter 20

ISN'T ANYBODY ELSE
LONELY LIKE ME?

A N EIGHTY-FOUR-YEAR-OLD LADY in Los Angeles once asked the above question to a newspaper reporter in the name of all of us. She put into words the isolated misery that grows like frost on the hearts of the lonely. There is no way to know for sure, of course, but people seem to feel that they are lonelier now than at any other time in history. "Bowling Alone" has become a famous essay because it speaks to our loss of community.

That, in part, explains some of the longing we often express for the times we never knew, those century-ago years depicted in Jane Austen or, so idyllically, in Currier and Ives lithographs. Life still exudes from those fine-lined etchings of contented-looking people who always seem to have the time to look at and listen to and smile with each other. But where is the time for all that now?

Our rapid pace and technology have produced a kind of progress, but they have helped to produce something else as well — a plaguing sense of loneliness that makes us feel fixed at isolated distances from each other like the figures in an Andrew Wyeth painting. "Isn't anybody else lonely like me?" the old lady asks. And the answer could be, "Yes, millions of us."

The tragedy of loneliness is that it is one of those human experiences that should really make us discover our kinship with each other. An elevator ride is often used as a model for the kind of journey we make through life. We all recognize the strange and somewhat oppressive intimacy of a crowded elevator. For a moment, sinking through the shaft of a great building, we are closer to each other than we would like, and we feel a tension that does not come just from the effects of gravity. We are uneasy and we are silent; we are not even sure where to look. So we hold our breath as we silently wait for the almost blessed release when the doors part again and we can pass out into the anonymity of the main floor crowds.

It is not strange that we have all experienced these pressures; it is just sad that we experience them separately — alone, each of us — while in reality we are all going through the very same thing. That is the way it is with loneliness in our world today — a common wound felt only by humans, a suffering that should make us less than strangers. We can all say with the old lady from Los Angeles, "If you are alone, you die every day."

Perhaps loneliness, that sheer and icy fortress, yields only to an increased sensitivity to each other, a heightened recognition of our similarities rather than of our differences. But it is a strange world these days, a world of separate self-definitions — black and white, ethnic and political, social and religious, correct and incorrect. These ancient strains have kept us separate but are now emphasized anew to make us more aware of individual dignity. And black is beautiful, there is no doubt about that. But I wonder if it would not be better to say that black is human; and so is red, and brown, and yellow as well. And, of whatever color, they all get lonely and discouraged and look for love, as do all persons who share the inheritance of the earth. We have a claim on each other in our common humanity, in the way we discover joy or sorrow, or know loneliness. This is the awareness through which we can lift away each other's loneliness.

Love, as we know well, conquers death, overcoming its curse and outlasting its pain. But love also conquers life. In many ways, that victory is just as difficult to achieve, because life wears a crooked and ambiguous smile that covers its contradictions and all its loneliness. Only a force as powerful as love can get us through a life that so often bows us to our knees and makes us cry out, "Isn't anybody else lonely like me?"

Chapter 21

LONGING

E VERY PERSON knows the experience of longing. We all long for many things in a lifetime, and, no matter what we acquire or achieve, the ache of longing is never completely eased. It is a sign of our continuing incompleteness; we cannot hold our most wondrous moments in focus for long; we cannot trap time nor stay change, the elements that eat away at every life; we move or are moved restlessly forward, always searching but never quite finding enough to fill ourselves.

Rachel yearned for her children who were no more, and Christ longed for the people of Jerusalem who would not hear him as he wept over that city. In every age people have longed for other goals: wealth through alchemy, an earthly paradise through voyages of discovery, and, in every age, especially this one, contentment through affluence and spirituality without struggle.

Humans only yearn more deeply as they face the disillusion of getting what they thought they wanted, or the disappointment of grasping at the mirages that dot the journey of life. It is never quite all there, and so we feel that we are never quite all there either. There is always a new challenge, a constant eroding of achieved securities, always a sign of our capacity for fulfillment and our failure to find the right formula for it.

We have abundant evidence of our incompleteness, of our openness to being filled, and of the impossibility of our ever being completely fulfilled in this world. So St. Paul could write of the cosmic longing in which we all have a share. "From the beginning till now the entire creation, as we know, has been groaning in one great act of giving birth; and not only creation, but all of us who possess the first fruits of the Spirit, we, too, groan inwardly as we wait for our bodies to be set free" (Rom. 8:22, 23). This is the restlessness of the heart of which St. Augustine wrote, the restlessness that is quieted only by God. Our longing is one of the "rumors of angels" that sociologist Peter Berger once described, a hint of the fulfilling God who lives beyond all our longing and who alone can respond to it.

This does not mean that humans cannot experience God's faithful response to their deepest longings in this world. Indeed, Christ promised life, "life to the full," to those who followed him. Our longing points to the level of experience in this life where the Spirit touches us and puts us in contact with the source of all life. This is the level of our relationships with each other, deep beneath the surface at which so many of our contemporary longings are pursued. Indeed, a person cannot even experience the real meaning of longing unless he or she gets inside life and begins to understand what it means to believe in and trust others and to find their own selfishness challenged and shattered by the challenge of hoping and loving.

The saddest part of our present plight is that we sometimes grasp at the shadows of superficial values in our quest for fulfillment. Our deepest longings, however, transcend the latest styles in clothes, cars, and acquisitions, great and small. Revealed are the emptiness of the current search for an erotic nirvana and the utter loneliness at the top that follows when people aggressively hunt for power. Such goals do not match the full dimensions of our nature, and so they multiply rather than relieve our longing. A pathetic footnote to this is the news that many men's magazines will not accept any advertising that makes men aware of their shortcomings. No ads spotlighting their frailty or their incomplete education can find a place in their pages because this might break the spell of sophistication and contentment that such magazines supposedly confer upon their readers.

Only real-life experience in seeking to love somebody else responsibly brings us an understanding of ourselves and the kinds of values for which we truly yearn, no matter how disguised our gropings may be. At the level of faith, hope, and love we know our greatest longing can receive our most fulfilling response.

It is also, of course, where we know our most painful disappointments. Believing, hoping, and loving bring us to life, but they also make us vulnerable as we can never be if we shield ourselves from these experiences. Because ordinary living can be so painful many people back away from it. Seeking to avoid hurt, they merely intensify their longing. Less important goals can be substituted readily but at the dangerously high price that these people may never know what life is all about.

A husband, for example, can replace his marriage with his job. He protects himself from facing the demands of loving his wife and children by plunging into work so that it keeps him at a defensive distance from them. So, too, a wife can find many distractions, including her job, to fill her calendar, but these may leave the core of her life quite empty and unexplored. Any of us can do this in a culture that proposes so many pleasurable distractions that they prevent us from ever knowing who we are and keep us from testing ourselves in the trusting and loving that give life its meaning.

It is the paradox of faith that it has always pointed to the only situations in life where longing can be overcome and that these situations are the most dangerous ones for us to enter. The paradox is heightened by the fact that life is given to others and attained by ourselves only when we are prepared to face pain and a special kind of dying.

A crucifixion is part of responsibly loving other persons, but this invitation to death is also an invitation to resurrection. We find life when we lose ourselves for the sake of others in the process. Longing for life and love is a signal that our fate is worked out in the dynamics of being ready to die to ourselves in order to find ourselves. That is how it works, and the only way it works. But selflessness and being ready to die are hardly popular commodities at the present moment; our flight toward fulfillment is in another direction altogether. It is an illusion as old as magic.

Our present worst peril is found in the ease with which popular culture provides us with a virtual life, the way it exempts us from facing the real issues of our identity as human beings. Self-understanding follows a painful path, and there seem progressively fewer willing to take it. The strange thing is the reverse paradox that is provided by this. The more we can have of the goods of life, the less we are able to deal with the riches of our own personality and the more we are estranged from self-understanding.

The more we want to avoid death out of fear, the less able we are to taste life. Somewhere deep down where the sparks of our humanity are still fiery bright we will be restless and wonder why. Inoculated against the deepest feelings of our nature, we long for them all the more. The cost of living becomes too high, but the price of longing rises higher still.

So Archibald MacLeish could write:

The crime against life, the worst of all crimes, is not to feel. And there was never, perhaps, a civilization in which that crime, the crime of torpor, of lethargy, of apathy, the snake-like sin of coldness-at-the-heart was commoner than in our technological civilization in which the emotionless emotions of adolescent boys are mass produced on television screens to do our feeling for us, and woman's longing for her life is twisted, by singing commercials, into a longing for a new detergent, family-sized, which will keep her hands as innocent as though she had never lived. It is the modern painless death, this commercialized atrophy of the heart. None of us is safe from it.

Longing remains a significant clue about us. It is not something to be smothered, or disguised. It reveals the depths of our nature and points to the equally deep level of experience that constitutes the ground of life. For the believer, it resonates with the Bible, gives meaning to hope, dares us to die for a fuller life, and opens us to the Spirit who really does offer us life to the full.

Chapter 22

A FEW KIND WORDS
FOR LOSERS

THERE IS NOTHING Americans love more, the old saying goes, than a winner. But where, given the relatively small supply of first places available, does that leave most of us who may not have the chance, the skill, or even the dumb luck ever to win anything except a bamboo backscratcher at a church bazaar?

Who, after all, wins the Lincoln Continental, the mink stole, and the trip for two to Europe and beyond? That's right; somebody who bought only one raffle ticket, the lady who has a mink stole already, and the same couple who won the kitchenful of appliances last year. But you? Never. Along with a large, shuffling, and anonymous army, you have somehow missed first-place money in all your years of going to school, playing amateur sports, buying chance books or lottery tickets.

According to legions of Americans who, admitting that they don't look like the late John Wayne, imagine that they at least sound like the late Vince Lombardi, winning is everything. While we like good losers, we don't make much room for them in our affections or our sports pages. But there is more losing in life than there is winning, and people who do not realize this just invite bitterness and frustration into their lives.

Furthermore, it may be that we have gone much too far in justifying almost any kind of behavior as long as it leads to winning. Lying, cheating, knifing others in the back in the climb to the top — we have had enough of these to last us until the next millennium.

On the other hand, we have been so disillusioned about the impossibility of winning at life and love that we now celebrate what we might call willful losers — non-heroes, drop-outs who reject life because they prefer to think that it does not really mean anything anyway. Such people flood our movies, our books, and, according to some accounts, our choicest national parks. Hard winners and born losers: They seem so different and yet a closer inspection reveals that if not blood brothers they are at least second cousins.

We all are familiar with those so wrapped up in winning or afraid of competition that they fix every outcome in some way or other. Fair fights, after all, are not for them; the end justifies the means, no matter how questionable the means may be. Such persons do not really face life on its terms but write their own scenarios, cueing the scenes so that the action works out the way they want it. In their hearts, you see, they are just deathly afraid of losing. And when, by whatever means, they win, they are deathly afraid that they will lose what they have acquired.

Drop-outs are terrified of losing too, terrified of showing that they care, and so they choose a course that protects them from failure by embracing failure as a vocation. These types are not very healthy or productive.

But other kinds of losers also exist, the individuals who believe in something and do their best to achieve it, even against great odds. They cannot always win, but they sleep peacefully because they live honorably. It is just that we have little time for these people, and too often not enough recognition of their integrity and their character. People who compete fairly on the basis of their convictions and from their inner courage may not enjoy the experience of losing but neither does it terrify or destroy them. They live by a mature set of values and offer us a model of the way people of faith do live.

These latter persons commit themselves to a course where they are always in danger of losing everything. This is the down-to-earth experience of men and women who try to live by the Spirit and who find that this frequently leads them along a narrow path where they are vulnerable to the massed forces of defeat and discouragement. Believers who are promised that their faith will overcome the world do not imagine that this will be accomplished through military conquest or some modern-day miracles that will astonish and humble everybody standing by.

They know, through the sort of wisdom wrought by the Spirit, that the world is overcome only by those prepared to lose themselves in loving and serving it. Believers possess the very things that everybody yearns for, the values that cannot be acquired by either the ruthless or the passive, the things you really do not lose even when you give them away.

Many people have indeed lost these qualities and cannot seem to find them again. Believers give of their belief to those who have lost faith in themselves, in life, in any kind of God; they give of their hope to those who have given up on finding any good anywhere at all; they give of their love to those who think they have lost it forever.

A deep and central element of the religious message is the spiritual mystery of being ready to die in order that others may discover life, being ready to risk everything, not foolishly or impulsively, but purposefully for the sake of other people. Those who insist on winning and those who insist on losing can never understand that at all. But this mystery, this incredible reality of the everyday spiritual life, is the great sign of faith that overcomes and reconciles the world at last.

Chapter 23

DOLDRUMS AND DEPRESSIONS

IT CAN HAPPEN at any season, but it often comes in summer. Just when we ought to be carefree, recovering from the long winter behind us and storing up energy for the season just ahead, we sometimes find ourselves suddenly and inexplicably down in the dumps. Everything can be going fine when, all of a sudden, we turn our head and the world looks different. The wind slackens and our sails collapse; what we had anticipated we now have little feeling for at all. We have filed for Chapter 11 of the Spirit. A seasonal illness, this specter infects us when we ease up a little, rising up to let us down right in the middle of our holidays.

There is nothing unusual about this kind of experience; it is the sort of thing we shrug off in the busier months when the clock leaves fewer hours for self-concern. The trouble with vacations is they give us time to worry about the things we don't have time to worry about during the rest of the year. Just let the days drag a little and we overreact to our little moods; we let them get the best of us or we throw ourselves too energetically into activity to combat them.

Wisdom lies in rolling with the emotional punches rather than shadowboxing our psyche, but there are also other lessons to be learned from a trip through the summer doldrums. Perhaps the first insight is to realize that these brief excursions into the gray fields of depression tell us what the experience of mental illness is like on a full-time basis for those suffering from it. We can read about it and listen to lecturers, but nothing will teach us more about emotional problems than to expand on our own intermittent brushes with them.

From this we get a taste of the way the world looks day in and day out for the people who are stricken by psychological problems that often seem so remote from us and always so difficult to understand. A little of that kind of learning is not a dangerous thing if it enlarges our compassion and helps us to realize that individuals with emotional problems are not like creatures from another planet whose experience is totally alien to us. What they suffer is an intensified and prolonged version of the "blahs" that we quickly try to kill off with distractions and pills. It is worth a little depression now and then to achieve an insight that helps us understand and relate better to the emotionally ill. They are not so starkly different from us after all.

The next time you sail into the doldrums, perhaps you can take some soundings of your own depression, be grateful that it is not so deep after all, and make room in your understanding for those who are over their heads all the time.

Chapter 24

DISCOURAGEMENT

N O EXPERIENCE is more common to us — none binds us more together humanly, than discouragement. It dries up a person's soul and seems to dig a crevice in every heart; it withers a spring garden like the biblical fig tree; the future that may have looked bright just a few hours before can be suddenly overrun with the black clouds of despair. Life does not come stamped with a warning label: You can be discouraged without warning.

Discouragement arrives like that, unannounced, unexpected, and quite unprepared for. We feel all the air drained out of us when discouragement suddenly overwhelms us. But discouragement can also be a slow draining away of our energies, the fibers holding the self together giving way, like those of a splintering barrel, only gradually. Either way, discouraged persons find that it is hard to keep going forward. In fact, so wearisome does life seem that they sometimes are not sure that they want to recover their strength at all. It is just too painful to return to the daily round with which they are so familiar — hard to get up in the morning, hard to smile, and hard to nudge themselves through the day, hard even to go to a sleepless night's rest.

Discouragement makes us want to give up and say, "To hell with it," about a whole variety of things in life: trying to do the right thing for ourselves and others; keeping at our work or keeping our promises; caring even for those we love with all our hearts, feeling that perhaps we are caught, random evolutionary bits clattering in a roulette-wheel life that may not have a payoff or even any real meaning.

Persons in the grip of discouragement do not respond to the smiling reassurances that shatter like glass as soon as they are uttered. They just crawl down more defensively into their personal darkness when somebody sings out, "Things aren't as bad as you think," or, "Don't feel so bad. Things are bound to get better." In their hearts they know these well-wishers are wrong, not because things won't get better but because of the false tone in their voices. The discouraged just feel more estranged when people offer them bluff heartiness as an antidote for the infection of garden variety, everyday discouragement.

Everybody knows that discouragement has a way of dissipating and we are sometimes hard pressed to explain why it does so. When it is heavy upon us, however, we need the presence of somebody other than the incurable optimist. We need someone who can truly be with us during the worst moments of our discouraged feelings, someone who can touch us humanly and be a source of hope for us. Some of life's more tragic scenes are acted out by lonely and discouraged people who have no one to share with them their empty and painful moments.

Persons who can make themselves truly present to someone in the midst of discouragement bring something deeper than easy reassurances. They bring more than the useless bromide, "I feel your pain." They bring the qualities that say, "I've been through this myself, I bear its scars. That's why I can be quietly with you in this discouragement and stay with you through it." People who can do this make a big difference in the lives of others. They deposit courage in accounts where it is overdrawn and breathe hope into others made breathless by visions of despair.

They literally encourage others because they put something of themselves into them. This encouragement through entering into another's melancholy does not take great training and it doesn't take very much time. It takes only minimal sensitivity to the human struggle, strength that comes from sureness about one's own identity, and a readiness to give ourselves rather than just good wishes to others.

There are people who feel too old or too shy to march, demonstrate, or volunteer these days, but who still want to make some contribution of service to the lives of others. They feel too self-conscious to be where the action is but they are ready to do something for their neighbor in a less dramatic and less publicized way. For these people (and for everybody else, of course) the opportunities to be sensitive to the discouragements of our fellows are everywhere. These may be found in our own families, in the lives of our friends, or among the lonely exiles in hospitals and nursing homes all around us. In an age when people are growing

weary of those who feel that relevance comes from tearing something down, being a source of encouragement to others is about
as positive a thing as a person can do. It is a way to love, a way
of making the Spirit present, of making spring come when winter
seems endless, and a way of giving life to those who need it more
than anything else.

Chapter 25

THE POST-DECISION BLUES

F OLKLORE TELLS US that we will feel better once we have made a decision about some important event in our life. "The worst is over once the decision is made," the sage tells us — whether what we decide is our major in college, our partner for life, or our job for the time being. After having weighed the alternatives and panned out the gold dust of our real motivations from the sand of our whims, we finally say this is it, this is the long-deferred moment of truth, the point where we finally commit ourselves one way or the other.

That should settle it, we feel, and so it does for many of the decisions we make in life. But there are other choices, with some of life's most important among them, that won't stay put; they keep wiggling in our consciousness, nagging at us and sometimes even presenting themselves once again, like the tax man for an audit, for a complete review.

The effect of finding a decision coming back for re-examination after we think it is filed away for good is disconcerting and even depressing. Did we think it over enough, we ask ourselves. Did we really take enough time with it? Only the wisest and most philosophical are immune from this kind of self-doubt, because they have learned that no choice is ever perfect, and they can live comfortably with that knowledge. Average persons are more vulnerable to wondering about their choices and, at times, a pencil-fine line runs between that and regrets.

Psychology, however, has discovered certain things about our decision-making processes, and a little knowledge of these can be a big help in handling the inner questioning that may persist after a big decision is made. A systematic tendency exists in all of us to begin to perceive more clearly the positive aspects of the alternatives we reject as soon as we reject them. It is a sort of over-the-shoulder-the-grass-is-greener syndrome. The person who buys house A, close to work and low in maintenance costs, suddenly see the advantages of houses B and C, freer of noise and air pollution, closer to resort areas, and near the new superhighway just announced for building out that way next year.

At the same time one begins to see more clearly the problems connected with the decision that has been made — the new lawn that must put in, the higher property tax, etc. This combination of awareness can lead us to sleepless nights, not because we have really made a wrong decision, but because we see the advantage-disadvantage quotient in a light that was unavailable to us before we made our choice.

In other words, the act of choice itself has this effect on us. We should not be surprised by it. Better, in fact, to anticipate this and be ready to take it into account rather than succumb to the distorted impression that we made a mistake. We will not be able to judge that accurately anyway until our time and distance perspective is much greater.

Our major commitments may, at odd times, thrust themselves up out of the sea of our consciousness like the Loch Ness monster: Is Nessie real or not? In strange and vagrant moments the decision opens wide before us again: Do I really want to go on loving this person? Do I really want to be a teacher anymore? Do I want to continue this career? Do I want to confirm the choice I made once, long ago it seems, when I was a slightly different sort of person than I am now?

Such internal questions bubble regularly around the issues that are most important to us in life. Those who deny that they have ever had these kinds of thoughts have just not been listening to themselves very carefully. For the big things ask us to choose them again, not to generate regrets in us, but to seek affirmation of ourselves in the deepest relationships of our lives.

It is the nature of love, work, and friendship to be open to our every new response rather than closed off as though they were not really a living part of us. "Once and for all," "Till death do us part," and "Now and forever" — these are some of our most profound phrases, but they take on their significance because they refer to relationships that by their nature demand that we keep saying yes to them as the years go by. It would be a strange relationship indeed, and not much of a one at that, that did not demand reaffirmation from us now and then.

Birthdays, anniversaries, and other ceremonials are our way of setting up occasions to underscore our life decisions all over again. So we go through our lives, ready to pull at the threads that forever hang loose from the choices we have made. We are less depressed by the imperfection of our decision-making when we realize that the condition is common and, in the most important parts of our lives, a good thing besides.

Chapter 26

THOSE HOLIDAY BLUES

S OME OF OUR DARKEST hours occlude the skies that should be the brightest. For example, nothing eats at our hearts more than the depression that suddenly overcomes us during the holiday season. Even when we have experienced the holiday blues before and try to keep on guard against them, we can find ourselves surprised and pushed by them into what seems a bottomless pit. All we know is that we are falling, that there are no handholds on the sheer siding, and that it will be a relief to hit bottom. It is that long slow fall into the depths that can turn a holiday season into a melancholy time and makes a dirge out of the music of celebration.

This is a common problem around Christmas time, especially during the letdown that inevitably comes after hard work at trying to make Christmas merry for everyone else. It may strike the father who has just assembled what seemed to be a thousand toys for the children he loves. Instead of being able to relish their enjoyment of them, he finds himself suddenly tired and depressed, as though a gauzy film of melancholy had dropped between him and his family. It can strike the mother, who having spent herself in getting everything ready for a good time, finds that she feels empty and unenthusiastic when she should be enjoying herself.

These depressions would be more understandable if one could point to something as simple and direct as the cost of the holiday shopping. They are not, however, related to the impending arrival of bills. Neither are they attached to illness of a physical kind, nor to some clear emotional disappointment. The holiday blues seem to settle on healthy people who cannot easily identify the reason for their sudden shift in mood.

It is reassuring to know that many people experience this kind of depression, and that it is not strange or unusual to find it in our own lives. It regularly visits people after they expend a lot of physical and emotional energy. It seems part of the strange feelings of anticlimax that human beings so often experience when they have looked forward to something with great anticipation. The event comes off and they go down, apparently deflated by the sudden relaxation of the tension that goes with achieving some goal.

So many weeks or hours are pointed toward this occasion that the letdown can be severely discouraging. This is intensified by its contrast with the general festivity of the season and our own inner expectations that we should feel better than we do.

Probably the best immediate antidote for the holiday blues is not another cup of eggnog but a frank admission of the way we really feel. We redeem ourselves when we stop demanding that we feel differently than we do and just accept the fact that, in the flawed human state, ups and downs are as natural as sunrise and sunset. I am not suggesting that we give in to the blues and thereby cause the disease to spread to those closest to us. It is helpful, however, to acknowledge our shift in mood and to examine it briefly to see if we cannot understand a little better the course of events that brought it about.

In that way, we possess ourselves more fully because we honestly face the state in which we find ourselves. Much better to do this than to try to hide our depression with alcohol, increased activity, or just a retreat into growling bad temper. The holiday blues always tempt us to let the Scrooge out of ourselves, something very unfair to those around us. At holiday times the latter are those we love most and are the ones we can hurt most easily when we don't even try to respond positively to this syndrome.

In any case, the holiday blues do not mean that we are sick. They mean that we are normal, that we are subject to the kind of swings in feeling that are common to all human beings, and that we would do well to face them directly and truthfully. We give each other an added holiday gift by vowing at least not to infect each other if the time-off blues settle on us. That may be one small step for us, but it is a giant leap for our family and friends.

Chapter 27

MAKING MISTAKES

IF THERE IS ANYTHING WORSE than making a mistake, the cynics say, it is getting caught at it. From the first time we are discovered putting our hand into a forbidden cookie jar to the last time we feel that sudden shock at seeing the state trooper in our rearview mirror, we know the experience well. We do not enjoy, and tend to suppress insofar as it is possible, those moments in which our indiscretion, bad judgment, or even simple human foibles are uncovered.

It is very hard to integrate our mistakes into our lives. We tend to disown them, to look the other way, and we certainly don't like to learn from them. If we did, we wouldn't keep making the same mistakes over and over again. There is something embarrassing, something deeply shaming in the uneasiness we can feel in our very bones when we commit a blunder. We do not like to admit it to ourselves because we might have to take a long hard look at it, acknowledge failure as something that comes from us and not from some mysterious source, and go on living as best we can. It is the stickiness of trying to unravel why we make the mistake, or continue to make the mistake, that is frequently the most difficult part of the whole thing.

We often get caught quite innocently, or so it seems, in the crossfire of events that show up our imperfections and inconsistencies. There are some situations, for example, in which it is hard not to make a mistake. So it is when we find ourselves under pressure from two friends who happen for the moment to be enemies of each other. Even in trying to help them heal their wounds, it is difficult not to step on some sensitive nerve endings. We sometimes despair of peacemaking altogether.

All too often the involved people end up mad at us rather than at each other. It is impossible to avoid such situations except through joining the government witness security program or falling off the face of the earth. The latter is the maneuver of choice when we try to do good and end up doing badly.

We need not, however, be innocent mediators to find ourselves mistake-prone. There is something in us that leads us, on certain occasions at least, to say the wrong thing, to laugh at the wrong moment, or to doze off when we should be alert. Making mistakes is really a part of every day's experience. It is no wonder that we prefer to remember the happy events of life and that we possess such powerful psychological mechanisms to blot out the things that are embarrassing. "Blessed are the forgetful," Nietzsche once wrote, "for they get the better even of their blunders." But it is not easy to forget our mistakes, or to live them down, and sometimes our regrets weigh us down and keep us from pursuing life as freely as we should.

If we stand back, however, and take a good look at ourselves, we realize that, before almost everything else, we are mistake-makers. We recognize the feelings of embarrassment and uneasiness that go along with errors because we all commit them so often. We are siblings in not learning from our mistakes precisely because we don't feel like performing post-mortems on them. We would rather just let them be buried and forgotten. It takes a genius, James Joyce wrote in *Ulysses,* to get through life without mistakes. But that is because the genius can turn errors into what Joyce calls "the portals of discovery."

Few of us can romanticize our errors as a great writer can. The best thing for us, then, is to approach ourselves with a little more understanding and a greater willingness to accept our imperfect state. Indeed, it is the fear of making a mistake that paralyzes some people so that they never use their talents very much in life at all. Not liking flaws in their performance, they hold back waiting for that moment or that time in life when they will get this down perfectly, whether it is speaking a foreign language, teaching a class, or giving a speech. At that far dawn, no one will be able to laugh at them and they will not feel that fast-spreading chill that veteran mistake-makers know so well.

But that perfect day never does come, not for any of us. In the meanwhile many people postpone getting into life until it is really too late. Then nobody cares whether they make mistakes or not anymore. The saddest graveyard is not that one in which our mistakes are buried but the one in which the talents of people who are afraid to make mistakes rest undisturbed.

Mistakes seem increasingly intolerable in the age of machines that are supposed to run so smoothly. I could not help but think of this after reading the scientific discussion in which so many eminent persons expressed concern about the scientific mistakes of one of the visits of humans to the moon. The rockets performed perfectly, the trajectories unfolding in accord with the mathematics that dictated them. The flight plan was a masterpiece of cool calculation. However, the scientists experienced disappointment because the astronauts were human beings quite thrilled by being on the moon.

Their vital exuberance led them, among other things, to ruin a television camera and to leave a large set of pictures behind when they took off. Men were dancing on the moon, responding to something deeply human, manifesting the wonderful unpredictability of our mistake-making. Such lunar mistakes are, I think, worth it just to hear the sound of human beings laughing on the moon's surface. It gives the rest of us mistake-makers heart. We can recognize our common-flawed humanity better as we watch people engaged in such cosmic playfulness. We are mistake-makers, we always will be, and the sooner we are able to forgive ourselves for it, the richer will be our enjoyment of life.

Chapter 28

DO YOU EVER FEEL RESTLESS?

NOT ALL THE PACING ABOUT in confined quarters is done by lions in their cages. Men and women do it all the time in the grip of a restlessness that just won't let them settle down. Symptom and response are curiously intermingled when the mood of restlessness is on us; we keep on the move in a variety of ways, and these movements are both signs of something out of joint inside us and the ineffective solution we try to apply to it.

When we are restless we find that it is difficult to concentrate on anything. We are always looking out the window, getting up to see if the mail has arrived, or perhaps rereading yesterday's newspaper, doing all these things with a studied but uncomprehending intensity. Sometimes we just drift around, feeling a little better as long as we are out of the chair in which we are supposed to be working, but not getting anywhere no matter how far we roam. Restlessness plagues the housewife, the bishop, and the executive indiscriminately. It makes them feel bad that they really don't feel better, and it causes them to look for little jobs to do when there are big ones waiting for them.

There are many reasons for this easily recognized behavior. But when the spirit of restlessness is abroad in the land, who can think hard or deep enough to analyze it? When somebody says to us, "What's the matter with you today anyway?" we are more than likely to answer, "I really don't know...," as we drift off to have another look out the window.

It may be helpful the next time these all too human symptoms reappear in our own lives to take a deeper look at ourselves to understand what is really happening. Restlessness ordinarily points to some unfinished business in our life, something with which we have yet to come to terms. As long as we delay the matter, or perhaps deny it altogether, there will be little progress elsewhere. Restlessness is one of the proofs that we cannot successfully dismiss or drown out what is really going on inside ourselves.

Restlessness, for example, can be the result of a frustration that we have pushed aside that still maintains an invisible grip on us. Restlessness can be a sign of foreboding, or it may result from some situation we do not want to face. It may point to a conflict, one that for some reason or other we really do not want to resolve. A man may have a disagreement with his wife that is unresolved as he heads off for work. It sputters and smolders and keeps him off balance all day. He may blame the weather or bad luck for his restlessness, but he will not understand the real reason until he recognizes and works through the difficulty with his wife.

So, too, people may be in conflict because they have a difficult choice to make such as changing a job or buying a new house. These decisions can sometimes be so difficult that it is easier to keep delaying them. Restlessness is merely the sign that we cannot successfully put off a conflict, that it is there, asserting and announcing itself, as all living things do. Sooner or later we must read the calling card it leaves in the silver tray of our consciousness.

Our restlessness may be an early reaction to something that is just over the horizon, a prophetic invitation to look in a new direction or accept a new challenge that has not quite formed clearly in our mind. Restlessness of this kind may tell us that there is not enough meaning in our life, or that our relationships are not as deep as we think they are, or that there is more to our potential than we believe.

It is good to look in one or all of these directions before we give up or merely seek out some diversion to distract us even further from the source of our restlessness. Restlessness, after all, may point us toward a richer, happier life if we follow it down to its real roots inside ourselves. It is never cured by a holiday; there is nobody as unrefreshed as vacationers whose restlessness makes the trip with them.

In the long run, restlessness says that we feel a ragged edge in life, that there is something in us that wants attention. We need not be geniuses or spend fortunes on psychotherapy to begin to understand it. As psychiatrist Karen Horney once wrote, "Fortunately analysis is not the only way to resolve inner conflicts. Life itself remains a very effective therapist." Those who search out the roots of their restlessness discover that a fuller, more honest facing of life cures it better than anything else. They may also learn that their lives can be far more wonderful than they ever suspected.

Chapter 29

THE LONELINESS OF BEING AHEAD OF YOUR TIME

PROPHETS ARE WITHOUT HONOR, they say, at least in their own country. But why is that? Why, especially in an age so fascinated with the future, should people turn their true prophets out to pasture and send their genuine seers into exile?

Wise men nod and tell you that it has always been this way, that there is no known cure for this malaise which has been fatal for so many who really are able to tell us what is to come. The cure is elusive because even though many relish scandals and bad news in the present they want to believe only good news about the future. People have been killing the messengers of bad tidings for a long time now, and prophets, because they bring bad news as well as good, are not much fun to have around.

Prophets are guilty of talking about things as they are, of describing reality as the collage of good and bad that it necessarily is; that is why they are unfavored by the people who do not want to see the world in good focus. Prophets are not magicians, readers of tea leaves, or searchers of the stars. They are the persons whose fundamental good sense and vision allow them to see deeply into people and events now; they can imagine well what people will do in the future because they understand them in the present. Human understanding, as any beleaguered government planner can tell you, is a far better guide for the future than growth curves and economic "game plans."

Well, that all sounds relatively harmless; no need to get upset over people with human insight. Therein, however, lies the rub, and also maybe the best way to tell false prophets from true ones. False prophets do not have the integrity of real prophets; they put on a good show, but they are fundamentally self-serving. Authentic prophets have too much integrity for that, so they just say what they sense to be the truth because they feel an overriding commitment to their own clear view of things. They can do no other.

This is exactly what gets them into trouble wherever they may be found, whether in religion, business, or public affairs. Prophets who know what they are talking about deal in truth, not public relations spin. They dare to put into words what most people, deep down inside themselves, are afraid to acknowledge as true. People do not want to face the truth that is too threatening to them. If they do, they will have to change and they are not ready for that at all. So it is easier to turn things outside of oneself, to project one's anger about an unfolding truth on the person who is brave enough to speak it for the first time. The prophet is not honored precisely because his or her vision of the way things are is too frightening, too demanding.

This is what Jesus did in his preaching, and why he was such a threat to the stultified religious establishment of his day; we are threatened by anybody who summons up the implications of our hardened hearts and human ways. They make us uneasy, not because they tell us about some science-fiction possibilities (the kind of acceptable and distant truth we swallow enthusiastically) but because they tell us what is really occurring in our own lives and our own times. People want a "new age" not a hard one.

Real prophets are dangerous because they take away our illusions and fragment our pretensions; they simply don't let us get away with anything. We can forgive others for many things, but we seldom seem to forgive another for being right when we are wrong. Hence the difficult state of prophets in their own country arises when they overturn cherished defenses simply by knowing what they are talking about.

You can find real prophets in any walk of life: in businesses that would rather fail than accept the truth about the future; in armies and navies that want myth more than reality; and in churches that preach harsh sermons but dread hard truths.

Maybe we should try to make life easier on prophets wherever we meet them. Of course, listening to prophets means that we must be ready to change ourselves, prepared to recast old beliefs and to integrate new aspects of reality into our worldview. Adapting might be quite hard on us at the start, but it could be very beneficial in the long run. And prophets, when we have the courage to listen to them without keeping up our guard, really know something about the long run.

The prophets who are very self-conscious about their predictions are very anxious to control our lives. They confuse rather than enlighten us, but the world listens to and regards them because they generally tell people what they want to hear. There is something of the "yes man" and the snake oil salesman in the false prophet. It is an old act even when it is called a new age. But true prophets are rooted so deeply in the truth that they know the direction in which it is taking us all. In prophets we glimpse something of the wonder of what men and women can be.

Chapter 30

POINTLESS MEETINGS/ WASTED HOURS

DO YOU EVER get the feeling at a meeting, or perhaps in a private discussion, that, despite all the talk, somebody, somehow or other, is managing not to get to the point? It is a strange experience for the direct and the sincere to find that the small sandbar of reason on which they are standing is slowly being worn away by a heavy tide of hogwash. At first it is hard to believe that a discussion, ostensibly called for a sane and useful objective, should be so deliberately and obviously frustrated. But it happens time and again in settings as varied as the Senate floor and your living room. Suddenly the least important subject gets extensive discussion, the clock runs out, and the serious question that brought everybody together in the first place never gets discussed at all. Why does it happen and what do you do when it happens to you?

Maybe we should review some examples. Did you ever attend a faculty meeting to talk about something important only to suffer through two hours about professors' parking regulations? Did you ever have some friend, desperation edging his or her voice, call you over at a late hour only to beat around the bush aimlessly after you arrive?

Car salesmen are masters at not answering direct questions, and manage to talk about something else when you are trying to find out what it is really going to cost you to get that new car. After many years they build a certain intimidation into their manner that makes the customer feel slightly apologetic for taking their time in the first place.

Nobody, of course, beats the Irish who, the legends tell us, learned circumlocution during the bad days when the English were always bearing down on them for this reason or that. We have all heard of the Irishman giving directions to the lost traveler. "If you want to get to Dublin," he says charmingly, "then it would be better to start from some place else." A friend of mine, worn out from trying to extract a yes or no from an Irishman, thought he had one cornered outside the famous Dublin Post Office. "Is that the post office?" he asked, sure that the answer would have to be short and to the point. But this was no challenge at all to the Irishman who replied, "Is it a stamp you want?"

But what do you do when you cannot seem to get anybody to come to the point, when you feel that one more moment of this kind of delay and you will surrender to unconsciousness? If you get angry you fall into the trap to which such roundabout conversations very often lead. You are then the one who breaks up the meeting, who makes it impossible for anything to be accomplished. You, who seem all innocence, are the villain. And it isn't very helpful to get up and leave, to heave an inkwell through a window, or to throw a punch at the man sitting on your left. That is the kind of fantasy this frustration induces in the normally calm and collected person who wants to find out only why the discussion or the meeting is not really getting anywhere.

One must turn to another level of speculation, the one a floor or so below the surface of events, where we are able to discover the explanation for why things are moving sideways instead of forward. Often enough, if it is a meeting, the issues have already been settled outside of it and nobody wants to discuss anything important because there is no point to it.

More often, however, the true problem is just too much for the people to deal with, even though they know perfectly well what it is. It is too much because they are the people responsible for dealing with it, and they cannot summon up the strength to respond. It is much better, then, to discuss some problem they can deal with, howsoever petty, rather than one they cannot deal with, howsoever real. All the distracting talk is a psychological camouflage that keeps you away from the important topic but also tells you quite clearly that for some reason or other this individual or this group is incapable of dealing with it at the moment.

There is not much percentage in trying to force the issue rationally because the actual obstacles are on the emotional level. Until these are dealt with there will be no progress made anyway. We only get more frustrated if we persist in trying to discuss what others are emotionally unprepared to talk about. Average persons do not find it easy to help others identify the emotional blocks that make them avoid the point of discussion, even though in the long run this is the very thing they must come to terms with. Better to save your breath or use your intelligence to try to fathom the level that tells you what is really happening, or rather, why nothing is happening at all. But do not try to apply reason. As the Irishman said, if you want to get to the point, it's better to start from some place else.

Chapter 31

BAD TIMES: HOW TO SURVIVE
A BAD DAY

B AD TRIPS, they said a generation ago, came from too much acid, but bad days have always come from too much of life itself. One may muse on what is so rare as a day in June but there is no such poetry connected with what is so common as bad days all around the calendar. February has a certain charm about it, probably because its brevity automatically insures that it will produce fewer bad days than any other month. No matter how you look at them, or try to avoid them, bad days constitute a rainy season in themselves and everybody gets soaked sooner or later.

Indeed, sometimes it does seem that bad days, when most everything goes wrong, are an external and impersonal force of fate with the power to darken the sun, to sour happy dispositions, and to staunch the flow of good news while they loose the floods of bad. They may fall on Monday, but it then really seems more like Monday falls on us. And there is no guarantee that the coming of Friday (as in "Thank God it's Friday") will mean the passing of bad days.

They pop up on weekends, holidays or, treacherously enough, during long-planned vacations. We know, of course, that these bad days cannot be some force outside of us, that they only seem that way, and yet it is hard to rid ourselves of the victim-like feeling that surges up when a bad day moves in. That is why we have perennially cursed the fates on the one hand while trying to placate them on the other with rabbits' feet and a wariness for walking under ladders or throwing hats on beds. Superstition and astrology have prospered because bad luck and bad days seem to act on us from the outside.

We know well enough our own internal reactions to bad days. When bad news comes in batches, we get very discouraged, feel very lonely and isolated, or just feel vaguely and unaccountably "down." Is life really meaningless, we ask, and is assisted suicide such a bad idea after all? These feelings are hard to shake off, mostly because they are hard even to look at in the first place.

Bad days bring out one of the differences between men and women. When a wife, for instance, has a bad day, she can really feel terrible; she can seem, with tears and all, barely capable of living out the next hour. She pours out all her grief to her husband, underscoring the hopelessness of the situation while he is still trying to hang up his hat. This has the effect of turning the day into a bad one for him.

He is supposed to be understanding and sensitive, to offer support and encouragement. Even as he does this, however, he seems to catch, as though it were an infectious disease, her depression and dismay. In short order, he is thoroughly upset.

Then the difference shows up; the woman recovers rapidly, the tears are dried and a spirit of fortitude returns. She soars while her husband remains down in the dumps. She is likely to say to him. "What's bothering you anyway?" and, for some reason or other, he never can explain, or perhaps even understand himself exactly what happened to him. All he knows is that he is suddenly in the middle of a bad day and it is hard to get out.

The truth about bad days, of course, depends on how we cope with the stresses or frustrations of the world in which we live. Some people do not respond very well to frustration. They lapse into restlessness or apathy as their style of handling life when their objectives are, for whatever reason, thwarted. Others turn to daydreams, finding in them a magic world of release from the complex reality of their everyday lives.

Still others turn aggressive, taking out their bad days on those around them with snarls and scowls. Some even turn back the clock, handling the frustration of bad days by behavior out of their own earlier days. This regression is evident in kicking inanimate objects, in getting sick, or in taking one's bat, in some symbolic fashion, and going home.

Familiar as these reactions to bad days may be, they are not very effective; in fact, they tend to make things worse because they just frustrate us more. Kicking things does not make the storm clouds disappear; feigning sickness postpones but does not eliminate confronting the conflicts of the day; withdrawing like a spoiled child may seem a short-term success but it is a long-term failure. The all-time classic treatment for the bad day syndrome is a self-administered dose of self-pity mixed with smoldering indignation that life "is unfair." This does not work very well or for very long either.

Getting high on self-pity is a passive and inadequate way of coping with the depression that almost always creeps in somewhere during a bad day. The first thing to do is make some effort to redeem ourselves from our troubles, rather than waiting for some deliverance from the outside. A good beginning is to listen to what is really going on inside ourselves. This is, more often than not, the key to why things suddenly go wrong for us.

When we identify correctly what we are really experiencing, we can trace down its origins and see the whole situation in a more realistic manner. It is frequently a small hurt, one that we do not wish to face or to admit to ourselves, that starts a bad day going. Once it is under way, a bad day, like an avalanche, gains lots of momentum on its own. That is an added reason for getting back to the basic cause of our discomfort. Once we isolate that, we can, if we are honest enough, prevent it from overwhelming everything else we do.

It is not easy to face our inner selves and call by their right names problems, some of which make us look rather small even in our own eyes. It is nonetheless, the first line of defense against bad days, because it locates the problem not in some cruel fate, but in our own reactions to the difficulties of life. If we persevere in facing our real selves in these moments, we actually develop our own maturity considerably. Our self-esteem increases as the truth of our picture of ourselves develops fully. We handle frustrations in an adult manner and no longer need to revert to some reaction out of our childhood.

It is particularly important for believers to keep facing the truth about themselves and to grow wiser in managing bad days. As St. Paul wrote to the Galatians with apparent sensitivity to their bad days, "We must never get tired of doing good because if we don't give up the struggle we shall get our harvest at the proper time." St. Paul really had lots of bad days, and he frequently recounts them for his communities to encourage them to keep steadfast in their faith.

You can sense that he knows all about bad days when he says to the Romans, "I cannot understand my own behavior. I fail to carry out the things I want to do, and I find myself doing the very things I hate." And how touching his remarks to the Philippians, where he lets them know how much their concern has helped him: "I have been through my initiation and now I am ready for anything anywhere.... There is nothing I cannot master with the help of the One who gives me strength. All the same, it was good of you to share with me in my hardships."

And so it is for all of us in the human condition. Finding on bad days that we do what we don't want to do, we must realize that we desperately need God's help and that the support of understanding friends means everything. We all have our share of bad days, and we must be honest with ourselves in dealing with them, knowing that, in view of the needs of the world, we cannot give up on doing good. Our own bad days make us more understanding of the bad days of others and more compassionate toward every person struggling to stand fast against the headwinds of life. Bad days help us to see each other as part of the same family better than most of the bad sermons we have heard.

Bad days, believe it or not, can have a good side if we take them as a challenge to see more of the truth about ourselves and to give more of ourselves to the service of others. It helps a lot to be able to laugh at ourselves once in a while, but we probably won't find this easy to do until we achieve a good measure of self-knowledge. Self-knowledge has the marvelous effect of helping us to see ourselves in the right perspective. And that frees our good humor.

One thing is clear: There is no cure for bad days any more than there is for the common cold. There are only more mature ways to handle them when they arise. Just learning this is a big help in learning how to survive them.

Chapter 32

AND BAD WEEKS, TOO

BAD DAYS do rise in the calendar regularly, trap doors through which we fall end over end during the daylight hours when nothing seems to go right. They are no fun but they are a lark compared with the curse of the bad week.

After all, a bad day is only a tough twenty-four hours, but a whole week makes life into a minefield from which there seems to be no escape. One could almost believe in the existence of meddlesome gods beyond the clouds who have had this giant economy-size misery on the drawing boards for some time, just waiting for the right moment, which for us is the wrong moment, to put it on the market. The bad week has arrived and, except for the Excedrin people, nobody but the grinning gods is happy about it.

To string together seven bad days is almost as hard as assembling a block of Fifth Avenue real estate. By the law of averages something good is almost bound to happen in the midst of even the worst days; a good meal, a ray of unexpected sunshine, a smile from a passing stranger, a daydream of pleasant release. The bad week allows for none of these. Things go wrong and they keep going wrong all through the seven-day period. Even Friday doesn't help. The bad week is not your common up and down brace of days; it is all bad, unrelieved and unalloyed. People have been sending in reports of bad weeks from all over the country.

You can tell that the new bad week has arrived because you need not ask people about it. They tell you right off, almost without thinking about it. "That was a bad week!" they will say, too worn out even to ask for a consoling drink, just intent on reporting that it is over and that they have somehow survived. Bad weeks have been a boon of sorts for those who wear sign-boards that read "Repent," but they are hell on people making investments, facing big decisions, or leaving on vacations.

Sometimes bad weeks are confused with the signs of the times. It was in a bad week recently, for example, that a famous preacher announced that he perceived the biblical indications that the end of the world is at hand. And you, what happened to you that week? Chances are that you would just as soon not talk about it.

The bad week is obviously a serious social problem, as bad as any form of pollution and dizzying in its prospects for misleading and discouraging all of us. The very fact that we know about the phenomenon is, however, a great help in itself. This knowledge will keep you from thinking that you are falling apart, selling your stocks short, or buying underwater land in Arizona. It might give you the courage to hold on because you recognize the face of the enemy and as a result you won't feel so isolated about it.

Maybe a spiritual view will help us to be patient with our bad weeks and prevent us from spreading the infection to the cheerful and innocent bystanders around us. In any case do not be too alarmed when your next malaise clings to you like big-city smog. The bad week has arrived and will be around for some time yet.

Chapter 33

FLIGHTS OF FANTASY

NOT MTV, surfing the Internet, not even the world of laptops can ever surpass, for vividness and variety, the continuous showings in the private theater of fantasy within each individual's mind. Even though colorful fancies dance in the heads of the most sober-looking people, few persons ever talk about them, even to themselves. We are not talking about fantasy as a primitive defense but as the color commentary of the healthiest life.

What happens in their fantasy life sometimes scares them, or makes them feel guilty, or leads them to think that they are very different from everybody else. Actually, vivid fantasies are something we all have in common; they are a sign of our relationship in the human condition and they may be more helpful than they are harmful to us. We all chew on what Shakespeare called "the food of sweet and better fancy."

There can, however, be something terrifying and isolating about the images that flash into our heads. There is, for example, a peculiarly disturbing quality about the wild visions that arise when we cannot get to sleep or when we are awakened in the small hours of the morning. At those moments we feel all alone in the universe except for these strange imaginings that would never enter our heads in daylight. Everybody experiences this, just as everybody plays the role of Walter Mitty at times. We imagine ourselves at the center of things, heroes who rescue the great man and then slip quietly away into the crowd without giving our name to the reporters. Yes, and we all know that fantasies can have a strong sexual coloring that, despite so-called progress in sexual understanding, still has the power to unnerve us.

Many believers suffer a great deal because they identify sexual fantasies with the phenomenon that was once described as impure thoughts. A great deal of false guilt arose because of the identification of these two aspects of our mental life. Fantasies arise spontaneously, forming themselves from bits and pieces of our conscious and unconscious experience. They cannot be turned off as automatically as a TV set. As a result those plagued with them may feel extremely guilty.

This experience of fantasy is quite different from some deliberate effort to generate erotic imagery. The latter is under our control, something for which we can be responsible. The unfolding of fantasy, however, can be as endless as it is uninvited. It reflects the many layers of our human personality and is not in itself either evil or harmful.

Indeed, fantasy is the real mother of invention. The limits of human progress, we are told, are the limits of our imagination. Even for ordinary persons who will never conquer any new worlds, fantasy can serve a very helpful function. It allows them to test out new solutions to their problems and to explore differing roles in their responses to them. Without imagination they could not anticipate the simplest of situations. Fantasy is also a kind of safety valve that allows us to drain off the accumulated tensions and hostilities of the day in symbolic form.

Fantasies, of course, can also tell us something about ourselves. Certain recurring patterns may give us a hint of what we are like deep down inside and how we really relate to other people. If we understand these patterns, we find the source of some of our frustrations. We are then less upset by them and handle them more constructively.

Fantasies not only help us to understand ourselves, but they also help us to understand other people. Without imagination, it would be impossible to put ourselves in the place of friends or strangers. With the common bond of our humanity, however, and the resources of our imagination we can enter into the world of other persons and see it, as it were, from the inside. Harnessing our fantasy to this use, we go a long way in developing a sense of true compassion and in breaking down some of the emotional bases of prejudice. Imagination is a powerful vehicle for transporting ourselves into the circumstances in which others find themselves. Imagination, guided by a sensible tradition of values, may be our most powerful weapon in overcoming the estrangement and loneliness that are so common in our own day.

We penalize ourselves if we do not examine the world of our own imagination or if we hold it at a distance because we are afraid of it, or think we are different when we are really just like everybody else. The healthiest people can at times have some of the wildest and most irrational fantasies. There is much comfort in understanding that we are not alone in this regard.

So, too, there is good reason for traditional caution about not losing ourselves in a world of fantasy. One of the biggest temptations for hardpressed men and women is to turn away from the real world and into one of images and shadows. We all recognize dreamy persons who never get their fantasies off the drawing board, the sad people who live with their private glass menageries. Sadder still are those who week to intensify their daydreams through drugs, or live in Cyberspace as a substitute for real life. Some refer to the latter as "R.L." and judge it only one of their options for existence. Sooner or later for these people the boundary between fantasy and reality becomes blurred and they easily lose their footing as well as any sure sense of themselves.

Fantasies are too common ever to be very terrifying. Most average persons are not trying to escape from the harshness of life through daydreaming or drugs, and most people do not try to generate erotic fantasies as the wallpaper of their complete inner lives. We would be a little more friendly and forgiving of ourselves if we recognized the very common nature of fantasy and how it can be constructive as well as harmful. Fantasy may be one of those signs that this life gives us once in a while about the wonders that lie beyond all our struggles and pain, the good things that the eye has not seen and the ear has not heard and that God has waiting for us in glory.

Chapter 34

DID YOU EVER
FEEL LIKE CRYING?

T EARS SAY A LOT, but sometimes they are hard to understand.
We can weep for joy just as we weep for sorrow; some people
weep at almost anything while others hardly ever weep at all. Tears
constitute a language we all speak with different accents and mean-
ings according to the complicated laws of how we have learned
to express our emotions. The French, they say, cry quite freely
while Americans shed private tears to express something very deep
in their lives. How can something so wrenching to the soul be
described as "having a good cry"?

The truth is, of course, that we have all felt like crying and we
know from experience that tears bear varied messages. They can be
the recourse of children who are on the spot — the defense against
adult questioning or accusation that wins them mercy rather than
justice in the small missteps of childhood. These tears must be put
away if a person is to move into maturity. Sadly enough, some
go on weeping the defensive tears of childhood for the rest of
their lives whenever they are in difficult circumstances. Such people
never understand grown-up tears, the tears that are much more
than the sobs of self-pity. We may all feel sorry for ourselves at
times, but if we are relatively mature we can catch our emotions
and save ourselves and others from the self-indulgent and wasted
tears we might otherwise shed.

Then there are crocodile tears, the manufactured tears of the
insincere and hypocritical. So, too, we recognize the hysterical tears
that well up from the sheerest surface of people's lives. They are
on view at every televised awards ceremony. They do not move us
because they do not come from the depths of those who shed them
so easily.

Tears in the mature person's life come at very deep moments of sadness and joy, on occasions of separation and reunion, whenever love shows through in life. Tears are above all a sign that we are alive, that the heart still beats because we care about someone or something enough to cry. Only the dead or the totally despairing have no tears. People who live with hope and trust can cry aloud; they are alive and know the meaning of love.

Some people hide their tears to show their strength; others keep their sorrow secret because weeping seems a source of shame for them; and heavy hearted are those whose eyes are dry because their wound is so deep that they cannot let the hurt out at all. The loneliest of us are those who have no one in whose presence they feel free to weep, no one whose responding love can redeem them from the sadness that has settled into their souls.

It is a hard thing to cry but it is not a bad thing. It is a tragic thing to cry alone because this means we have built walls around our lives so high that nobody else can see over them. Our tears not only express the deep wells of our feelings, but they also make us one with everybody who has ever loved or tried to reach out in a tender and caring way to anybody else. Our tears, Dickens said, are "rain upon the blinding dust of earth, overlying our hard hearts." Our tears redeem us when they reveal us clearly to another, unshielded from the consequences or risks that are involved in being human.

If we have cried ourselves, we find something of ourselves to give back to the suffering and sorrowful all around us. We need not move away from them, bidding them to hide their tears because they hurt us so much. We have gone along the same human path and we understand how, in our grief, the presence of another person can bring a certain wholeness to our sorrow. We give life when we learn from our own weeping how to give ourselves with gentleness and compassion to the sighs and struggles of other people.

The psalmist was no stranger to weeping and neither was Christ, who cried over Jerusalem and at the death of his friend Lazarus. St. Paul tells us that the whole earth groans and cries out, longing for fulfillment. Mature tears are signs of the same kind of longing, a kinship with a world as yet unfulfilled. Our tears tell us that we still live, that we have roots in the lives of others, and that we are touched by the warmest of suns, human love. We should resolve that nobody we love every has to cry alone.

Chapter 35

FORGIVENESS:
THE HARDEST THING
OF ALL FOR US

L IFE IS SO FILLED with hard things, misplays and misunderstandings of all kinds, that it somehow does not seem quite fair that, on top of these, we are expected to forgive others for their faults. People prefer "getting even" these days or revenge, served best cold, as they like to say, the social equivalent of capital punishment in dealing with those who have wronged or hurt them. As we understand that familiar impulse we also grasp the immense demand that genuine forgiveness makes on us.

It cannot be forgiveness just in words; it has to be real or it does not work at all. Forgiveness, according to the Bible, must come from the heart and that, of course, is exactly what makes it so hard. When we do something from our heart we do it with our whole person; it is the moment, if the moment is ever to come, when we make ourselves fully present to others.

Forgiveness cannot coexist with closing off some inner chambers of personality in which we can keep the fires of bitterness banked until some opportunity for revenge comes our way. But we humans like to do just that, holding on to old hurts long after everybody else but ourselves has forgotten them, warming ourselves with the knowledge that we have kept some things on file for that great getting-even day. For some of us that makes all the suffering worthwhile. We can wait, like the Count of Monte Cristo, until that moment of freedom when, blinking into the sunlight, we can take out after our enemies.

The hard part of what Jesus said about forgiveness is that we must forgive them even when we are right. Forgiveness would not make much sense any other way, of course. It is not something for those who never hurt us but for those who do. It is hard enough at times to love our friends, but the thought of forgiving our enemies is downright startling.

That is what makes his teachings so extraordinary. He doesn't ask us simply to put up with and accept life's betrayals through some kind of sweet and quiet contemplation; he challenges us to be active, to go out and meet our enemies, not to spite them, but to embrace them. It is in the question of forgiveness that we experience down deep just how much genuine faith asks of us. It is anything but easy. There is no need for any self-inflicted mortifications in the true asceticism of such belief; just facing into the death that forgiving others demands of us is plenty.

Furthermore there is a real dying to self in accepting bad feelings as a part of ourselves. We like to skip over the mistakes and sticky episodes of life, not inspecting them too closely because it is too painful to do so. Self-examination comes hard especially in the situations in which we have been hurt. We do not feel much inclined to sort out the tangled feelings strewn across our soul like live wires.

We cannot be forgiving, however, unless we first admit that we can be vengeful and hard of heart. We do not even experience our own personality unless we take a close look at those parts of ourselves that we would ordinarily prefer to disown. We would rather push these feelings down or hide them in a haze of forgetfulness. But then we are only trying to bury a part of ourselves. It is from that grave that ghosts arise, specters that have power only when we leave them in the darkness.

Forgiveness of ourselves, it is commonly said, is necessary before we can forgive anyone else. This begins by admitting just how complex and contradictory we can sometimes be in our personal relationships. Forgiveness starts when we recognize the fullness of our faulted selves in the human condition and do not turn away. Forgiveness is accomplished when we can take responsibility for all that we are.

A marvelous freedom comes to us when we possess courage enough to see ourselves pretty much as we are. This freedom gives us the capacity to forgive others, a moral authority that springs from the love itself, the love that comes into life when we are truly in touch with the persons we are. Only such love enables us to redeem ourselves and others through forgiveness tempered in the cleansing fires of self-examination and self-acceptance.

For most of us this kind of forgiveness remains an ideal that we work toward throughout all our days. The pursuit of the fullness of forgiveness of ourselves and others is one of the signs that we are living and growing spiritually. When we forgive ourselves for the fact that it is necessary for us to keep working at this virtue, we take a big step closer to achieving it.

Chapter 36

TWO THINGS YOU CAN'T DO WITHOUT: FREEDOM AND TIME

THERE ARE TWO QUALITIES or conditions (call them whatever you want) essential for the most important things in life. They are also the two factors that many people count as enemies and so struggle throughout their lives to overcome them. We do not need wealth, comfort, or even good dreams to get through life; we have even less need for fame or good looks. What we cannot do without, however, in our most vital human experiences, are freedom and time.

Nothing that is humanly worthwhile can be accomplished outside the demands that these qualities impose on us; yet they are also the realities that frustrate us the most. There are legions who would limit a person's freedom; sometimes we even do it ourselves. And there are many who are unfriendly to time, uneasy and never at peace with the clocks that measure our days.

We cannot achieve anything of value unless we invest it with freedom and allow it the kind of time it needs fully to develop. All the things that season our character — love and trust, friendship and faithfulness — must come freely through the medium of time or they do not come at all. All life moves toward freedom, toward a healthy and responsible independence achieved only by those who commit themselves to a participation in the sacred mystery of time. Nothing that is ultimately good comes in chains or outside of time.

Even lovers whose hearts beat to a timeless pulse and who long for union must finally work out their relationship in freedom and patience. In patience, the scriptures tell us, we shall possess our souls. So it is for lovers who, anxious to lose themselves in each other, come up against the reality that they can never completely do this, and that the miracle of love exists only for people who recognize and respect their own separateness.

Lovers do break the barriers of time but time waits and reasserts itself and has its way with them. They cannot conquer or tame its effects with make-up, or fool themselves into thinking they have escaped at jet speed. A life worth living is one worth growing old in; lovers learn that doing this together is bittersweet but it gives full growth to their love.

It is surprising that we rebel against those perennial forces that are essential to fully human lives. Sometimes we want to control our lives and program our futures at the high price of eliminating all surprise. Worse than this, some people want to control the behavior of others; this great temptation comes, I suppose, to everybody who has ever loved anybody. We would like the beloved, in some wild and impossible dream, to remain unchanged, to stay forever youthful and forever innocent.

Parents can wish this for their children, teachers for their pupils, and even lovers for each other. This hint of the desire to prolong youth goes against the whole thrust of the human condition; it is a vain and betraying wish in the lives of those who try variously to carry it out. We may wish that those we love not change so that we will not be hurt by the changes that inevitably come if we allow our beloved to be free and subject to the measure of time. Wherever there is time, Joseph Campbell has written, there is also sorrow.

A double vulnerability is involved in letting people be free and allowing them to have their own lives in their own time. They may disappoint us or cause us pain because they use their freedom poorly or because they grow old when we wish they would not. We may, then, be inclined to overprotect our children or to isolate our loved ones from any opportunity to taste life itself. Controlling the lives of others or attempting to eliminate the necessary conditions of life are strategies that almost always diminish rather than enlarge the possibilities of the other.

What individuals need most are the freedom in which we stand by them and the time which we are willing to enter into at their side so that they can find and live by the truth of their own personalities. Freedom and time can seem like masters to us if we are afraid of them; they are on the side of those who have truly learned to love.

That is the problem with people who have no patience with the good things that insistently demand an investment of time. They want things immediately and the delay of gratification seems sinful to them. What is it, after all, that we can have right away in this world of wonders? Radios, televisions, electronic devices of all kinds coming immediately to life to tell us the news that we have already heard two or three times before, or bursting into color at the touch of a dial, to show a rerun of a game show? Our marvels of communication only make life more painful, seeding us with a greater yearning rather than satisfying us. The things we can have instantly are often shallow and insubstantial, commodities that cannot last and that quickly dissolve the very quality of time they attempt to overcome.

Timeless and lasting is a life to which we give ourselves freely in the knowledge that we must deal with time if we are going to live as God's children. There are a thousand deaths involved in tackling life on its own terms, yet these deaths give us more life because through them we discover the richness and the values of loving and believing that outlast all the clocks of the universe.

Believers commit themselves to the human condition, acknowledging their mortality and exposing themselves to the hazards of real living that scare those who are afraid of freedom and time. Spiritual values are eternal but they are rooted in a feeling for freedom and time. The Bible is full of the talk of waiting — waiting for the seasons, waiting for the harvest — rather than hurrying things beyond the tempo of their inner promise.

Coming alive is not accomplished in an instant; grabbing at it only betrays those who, despite their bright banners and balloons, have never learned to wait. Believers enter life accepting the responsibility of freedom and the penalty of time. Eternity offers the realization of the other side of freedom and time, that is, life to the full sealed forever against the vulnerabilities of our human passage toward it.

Chapter 37

WHAT'S WRONG WITH SAYING, "I DON'T KNOW"?

A LITTLE CON MAN dwells in the best of us, and he emerges at those times when we don't know what we are talking about. Most of us, of course, want to appear knowledgeable and, to some degree at least, sophisticated. Ah, to be somebody on the "in"; that same little urge leads us to exaggerate, fabricate, and generally misinform the world around us.

How many of us there are who reflexively employ certain phrases that seem to cover our ignorance and make us appear well-informed and in good control. For example, during the stock market slides people who have trouble balancing their checkbooks call upon the phrase "technical correction" to explain the situation. The wonder of phrases like this is that they make you sound intelligent and they discourage your hearers from asking further questions because they do not know what a technical correction is either.

The same kind of thing leads a person to diagnose any and every automobile problem with the words, "It's probably the points." This phrase has a gritty, manly quality to it and could seemingly be used only by persons who have travelled to the far reaches of the masculine game preserve and come back with the trophy of manhood.

Then there is the medical phrase that makes you actually feel you are wearing a white coat with a stethoscope draped around your neck, that phrase that we can apply to everything: "There is a lot of that going around this year." Many years ago comedians Bob and Ray gave their annual medical award to the doctor who first uttered these now famous and useful words. In fact, the words do seem to have a semi-curative or calming effect on the sick over whom they are uttered.

We don't need a stock phrase, of course, to release the con man in us. Sometimes all we need do is to nod our heads and grunt in varying tones of agreement or disagreement. There are times, also, when we go way beyond this and, through more active storytelling techniques, let people think that we have knowledge that we do not really possess. That can get us in pretty deep and we have a very difficult time extracting ourselves while at the same time preserving some measure of our dignity. In the long run, the momentary delicious feeling of being on the inside and being competent gives way to uneasiness at keeping the threads of all our claims pulled together.

There is, therefore, something refreshing about the person who can say, "I don't know," when that is actually the case. What comes through in persons like this is their genuineness, and this makes up for many other shortcomings. Only persons with very deep needs to impress others must say something on every subject, precisely because they are always involved in proving themselves. Research on human relationships shows that few things are more destructive than pretense. In the same way, nothing is more helpful than the simple truth, even when it is only an admission of ignorance. In friendship, psychotherapy, or marriage, not to mention the courtroom, the truth is much better than the urge to con the other person into thinking we know something when we do not.

The truth can hurt, and people can unwisely use it at times to inflict pain or put somebody in their place. I am not talking about that as much as the more familiar and less hostile tendency to think that the truth will not be good enough and that we must substitute something fancier in its place. People who do this habitually are afraid that others will consider their real selves inadequate and will reject them because of it. As a matter of fact, others despise their phoniness much more than their ignorance. We get by only with what is real about us. Friendship and love develop out of what is genuine about us in relationship to others. Con men end up conning themselves into terrible loneliness. So watch out, because there's a lot of that going around.

Chapter 38

GRATITUDE: LOOKING AT EACH OTHER

W E ARE, each of us and all together, so distractible, or so lost in our own dreams and plans, that genuine gratitude is sometimes hard to generate and even harder to come by. Christ found that out the way most of us do, in human experience, when only one of the ten lepers came back to thank him for having been made clean. We are a funny race, we humans, always looking for something for ourselves, sometimes missing the best things when we have them, and often too preoccupied to think of saying thanks for anything. If the Jesuit poet Gerard Manley Hopkins could "praise God for dappled things," perhaps we can find time to praise God for the simple things, most of them dappled, too, that are also the most profound things in life.

It is an old idea, of course, to remember that the stars and the sky belong to us all, as do fair days and first snowfalls. What we forget sometimes is that the real meaning of life is found on this quite common round of our experience, and we need the time and occasion to put this truth into perspective again. The only really poor people in this world are those who shield themselves from life and, because they are not really a part of it, can never give thanks for or celebrate it.

Not many people enjoy lives marked with high adventure or notable achievement; very few become famous or have monuments of gratitude raised in their names. The just go along, doing pretty much the same thing every day, dulled sometimes by the routine that is really the setting for the richest of all human experience.

Against that homely background of everyday life, people believe in and trust each other, they love and give life to each other, they try to do their best and leave things better for their children and grandchildren. Love, not fame or popularity, bridges the gaps of life and makes whole the lives of good people everywhere. To be present to each other in really sharing life is a far greater accomplishment than almost anything else that can be imagined.

Those who enter into the undramatic and everyday tasks of getting to know each other better, or raising a family, or serving others less selfishly: These same people know that these experiences constitute the texture of life itself. They also understand happiness and how much there is really to be grateful for in life.

We need to see each other afresh and to realize how much of the mystery lies in living together. We take it all for granted and forget what gratefulness is for; we are so busy planning for the future or regretting the past that we often miss the quickly passing moments of sharing and struggle that are at the very heart of life. Love is not found in moments of high romance nearly as much as it is in times of simple sharing.

That is what Thornton Wilder, the author of *Our Town,* was getting at with his story of the day-to-day life in a little New England village. In one scene after her death, Emily, the young girl, learns that if she wishes she may return to life again. She is warned by the others in the cemetery that it will be a painful journey, but she selects a happy and ordinary day, her twelfth birthday.

The stage-manager-narrator warns her. "You not only live it; but you watch yourself living it.... And as you watch it, you see the thing that they — down there — never know. You see the future. You know what's going to happen afterward." Emily returns and speaks to the recreated past that cannot hear her, the past where people are going about their everyday tasks: "Oh, Mama, just look at me one minute as though you really saw me. Mama, fourteen years have gone by. I'm dead, You're a grandmother, Mama.... Wally's dead too.... We just felt terrible about it — don't you remember? But, just for a moment now we're all together, Mama, just for a moment we're happy. Let's look at one another...."

Without too much self-consciousness perhaps we can look at one another gratefully, if only for a moment. We can celebrate how much we share God's goodness in the love that makes us mean something to each other. We can recognize that the life of the Spirit is lived only in the regular round of trying to love each other a little more. We may not be able to keep this view of things in focus for long. To do so even momentarily, however, places the real values of life back into perspective for us. It is a simple vision but it is enough to move us deeply, enough to make us join with Emily who said, "Oh, earth, you're too wonderful for anybody to realize you. Do any human beings ever realize life while they live it? — every, every minute?"

Chapter 39

CAN PRAYER BE AN ESCAPE?

THIS SEEMS LIKE a terrible question, worse even than questioning the importance of motherhood or the American flag. But then even these sacred cows have weathered some harsh seasons recently and have survived. Prayer, however, is always good, or so we imagine and so we are expected to say. We hesitate to criticize prayer because we see it as the work of the Spirit and count ourselves blessed if we are able to pray sincerely at any time. My intention is not to question that very broad category called prayer. Rather, I am wondering only about the widespread resurgence of interest in prayer, houses of prayer, and the experience of shared prayer advocated by professional religious figures, the increase in the number of "desert experiences" and other getaways of the spirit.

This impulse must be carefully evaluated precisely because it seems to be so unquestionably good. Whatever is truly of the Spirit stands up under close scrutiny; you cannot harm the things of God by inspecting them. The problem is that prayer, along with other forms of piety, is the most socially acceptable shield we have ever known for a retreat from the problems of life.

Some people have always knelt in churches, even in that distant time known as the Age of Faith, because they were afraid to stand up to what they might find outside. Prayer, that heightened relationship of the believer to God, has more than once appeared in counterfeit form; it has been used by madmen as well as mystics throughout the history of the world. In other words, we may be tempted to return to prayer in our day because, in spite of all our enthusiasm for reform and renewing the face of the earth, we find that this world is hard to budge. It is a stark truth that real religious influence, rather than an extremist caricature, is minimal in many quarters, even in certain parts of the church itself, and that it is not an easy task to preach God's word to the modern world.

Prayer looks even better to us when we play our trumpets but the walls of the world's cities do not crumble before us.

The late longshoreman-philosopher Eric Hoffer put it well: "How much easier is self-sacrifice rather than self-realization." It is much more difficult for believers to grow fully mature than to turn aside and ask God to finish work that proves difficult. There is, of course, no growth in faith at all without the aid of the Spirit. We run the risk of reverting to a childish prayer when we are frustrated by the severe nature of the challenges of adult living. Prayer by rote, devotions centered on the self, the quiet remove of a chapel visit — these are wonderfully comforting for a person who discovers the difficulties of standing up to an unforgiving world.

We need prayer insofar as it defines our lively and true relationship with our Creator. God, however, does not disappear if we do not think about him. God will not feel slighted, even if, out of pursuing justice and truth, we forget to say our prayers. But aren't these tasks very difficult to accomplish and thus isn't the idea of praying for their fulfillment intrinsically attractive? Isn't that what we are supposed to be doing, praying for everybody everywhere? Who can fail to give us high marks in faith if we are saying our prayers regularly? Perhaps our interest in prayer demands that we carefully check our own motivation lest this be some kind of cop-out on the enormous unfinished work of doing good when evil remains a formidable adversary.

Real prayer has never been and is not now an escape. Real prayer rises out of intense action, like mist from a fast-flowing river. It goes along with and develops out of a vital relationship to a world that is struggling and suffering to make itself whole again. Genuine prayer never invites us to turn away, not even at a slight angle, from the anguish of the world to which the Gospel is meant to be preached. We may have to learn how to pray less as innocent children and more as adults bloodied by life. The world can be mean, yes, and we have a great distance to go. Along the way, though, we had better be sure that our interest in prayer deepens rather than dilutes our commitment to solving the almost impossible problems of the human family.

Chapter 40

THE PSYCHOSOMATIC SIGNS
OF HEALTH

W E AMERICANS LOVE to take our own temperature, check our blood pressure, and generally keep a wary eye out for the signs of illness. We are interested in what we can catch and what we can prevent. It is not uncommon for persons to read a vivid account of the symptoms of some disease and then to find themselves experiencing these very things. Our imagination never sleeps but constantly plays these phantom pains and aches in the virtual reality of our heads.

We Americans have, in fact, become somewhat sophisticated in understanding the meaning of psychosomatic illness. We realize that the uneasy stomach and the blinding headache may have their roots in unsettled emotions rather than in some fault in our physique. We love this double feature of possibilities.

Bombarded with reports from every side, we are very conscious of the signs of distress and strain in our physical make-up. And we try every remedy in our never-ending pilgrimage of self-medication. We even freely exchange medicines with friends and neighbors. Perhaps it would be good to focus, as an antidote, on the signs of good overall adjustment, the symptoms of psychosomatic health.

The biggest indication of health is a lack of self-consciousness. Healthy men and women are absorbed in living and are not obsessed with concern for their own well-being in any exaggerated way. Indeed, good adjustment is never self-preoccupied. In the healthy individual the physical and emotional aspects of personality fit together to make a seamless whole. A general feeling of well-being is the result.

A further symptom of healthy individuals is found in their productivity. They reveal a certain zest for living; they are spontaneous in their capacity to work and in their relationships with others that is not a forced gaiety but the realization of their real creative possibilities. Healthy persons meet life and labor with an enthusiasm and anticipation that revivify and refuel them even as they carry out demanding tasks.

Healthy persons are creative in many ways, even in situations unrelated to the arts. There is an element of creativity in the healthy housewife, the busy priest, the interesting teacher, or the good neighbor. Creativity is not always dramatic, and it is an unproven if semi-popular notion that it arises only out of some kind of mental illness. A fresh approach, an ability to see things and people in a new light, a capacity to balance opposites, tasks done with pride — these are the blooms of creativity in everyday settings.

Close and affectionate relationships with other people are the prime signal of healthy personhood. Once again, this need not be excessively dramatic and is never hysterical. Reliable friendships, the ability to trust, the willingness to share oneself with others: These commodities come in different sizes but their source is the healthy personality. Well-adjusted persons love themselves properly and so they can be themselves in relating to others. You can identify this in their ability to receive and bestow love. Only unhealthy persons, lacking self-esteem, cannot effortlessly offer their real selves to others and cannot comfortably afford to receive their affection in return.

Adequate self-knowledge enables healthy persons to accept themselves as they are. They are aware of their feelings and the reasons for their actions and do not distort them defensively. They can accept their own imperfection as well as that in other persons and in the world itself. Healthy persons assess their strengths and weaknesses, know what they can do and what they cannot do, and, as a result, set realistic goals. They neither overestimate or underestimate themselves in the face of life's tasks. That is the healthy strength that makes them productive.

Perhaps, in the Space/Information Age when bad news bears down heavily on us, we should pay attention once in a while to the soundings within us that affirm what is right about us in the human condition. None of these characteristics is possessed in absolutely perfect form by any of us. They are, however, the kinds of experiences of the self that all healthy persons possess in greater or lesser degree. Loving ourselves properly includes a willingness to accept the good things about ourselves without making a big deal out of it. That is the best sign of all of our good health.

Chapter 41

BLESSED ARE
THE UNSELFCONSCIOUS:
THEIRS IS THE KINGDOM
OF HEAVEN

A T ONE POINT, the shining goal for many faiths and many cultures was perfection of soul. To this end, people strenuously practiced spiritual exercises to prepare for what they often termed the "combat" of purifying themselves of such things as "the desires of the flesh." That was all part of what some recall nostalgically as "muscular Christianity."

This has largely fallen away, as has almost all public speech in our country about the spirit or the soul. For many Americans, the goal now glistens as perfection of the body. The activity remains strenuous, although personal trainers have replaced spiritual directors and grunting at health clubs has replaced praying in silence in churches or temples. Control of the desires of the flesh has been modernized and legitimated as the elimination of body fat. While the vanquished body was once anointed for passage into eternal light, now it is oiled up for presentation under a temporal spotlight. Thus the pseudo-Eucharist of the age is celebrated as men and women proclaim, "*This* is my body."

While the spiritually ambitious entered the desert alone to encounter mystery and taste transcendence, now runners, as gaunt and unsmiling as those long-ago monks, flood the streets single file to hit the wall and enter the zone that is their promised land, or, excuse me, jogging path.

Churches are now locked up during the day to protect them from thieves who would break into their poor boxes or transients who would sleep in their pews. The church's function is carried out now in organic food stores, open at all hours, offering substitute mysteries at high prices. These people are not in the food business but the religion business, preaching near eternal life to those who eat immaculately conceived foods that have virgin birth at their table.

It is no accident that these seemingly different activities share such similar ideologies, vocabularies, and practices. In the name of hallowing and honing the self, those who make these tasks a way of life instead of just part of it pit themselves against their own bodies, counting loss to the latter as little in comparison with the gain thereby achieved. Both discount the incidental, but often permanent, damage they do to themselves in these parallel searches for perfection.

One wonders if these athletes, one of the soul and one of the body, are not really twins separated at birth, far more alike than different in their striving. If they represent the ideal, are we, who fall so short of it, predestined to damnation, out of shape and out of heaven for all eternity?

There is something intimidating about such far-out saints and strongmen. There is often something grotesque as well, as if the end product of their ceaseless sculpting of themselves internally and externally finally makes more a sacrilege than a celebration of human possibilities. The Frankenstein story survives not because it tells a gross tale of making monsters out of something else, but because it subtly recounts how we can make monsters out of ourselves. That is exactly what happens when men and women enter the Olympics of the spirit, competing to see who can eat the least, sleep the fewest hours, utter the smallest number of words, in order to achieve what they think is the goal of holiness.

The final state of such individuals is sometimes worse than the first because, like extremist body builders who mate themselves to Nautilus machines and long ago forgot what any food eaten by ordinary mortals tastes like, they begin to bulge and become top-heavy, and like the toy figures in the battery ads always seem about to topple under the burden they have fashioned out of themselves.

Self-consciousness reigns for those who excessively seek perfection and utter purity for either soul or body. Perhaps that is why overzealous muscle men can't live without mirrors and overreaching saints couldn't live with them. Self-consciousness is the worm that devours from within the apple of real health of soul and body.

Perhaps the most distinguishing sign of genuinely good—to use a more modest term than holy — men and women is their lack of self-consciousness. They are not self-conscious because they forget themselves whenever they respond to others. They are not always thinking of how they look, what others will think of them, whether they eat in a politically correct way, or whether their clothes and make-up will be right for television. In short, these people may forget a lot but they remember how to be human, which may be defined as being imperfect with grace, which is very different from the graceless, and sometimes ruthless, hunt for self-conscious perfection in the gym and whole food temples of our times.

The gracefully imperfect, the authentically holy people of our time, are to be found all around us. They show us how to live by living without obsessing about it all the time; they teach us how to love because they don't set out to teach us anything. In a manner that recreates the simplicity attributed to real saints, they endow familiar gestures with extraordinary and moving nobility, as a parent does by gently pulling the blanket up on a sleeping child, or neighbors do who stay up all night with us when someone is sick or there is a death in the family.

In their most wonderful revelation about the nature of sanctity, they transcend themselves, without even knowing it, in emergencies. Thus, after disasters, natural or unnatural, heroes arise, as saints are supposed to in bleak times, and then disappear once again, as saints are also supposed to, into the ordinariness of their lives.

The moon is an extraordinary symbol because it rises and dies in our very sight; it gives itself to the darkness and finds itself once again flooded with light. Scientists have suggested that the moon saves the earth by preventing it from wobbling out of orbit. That is the way really good people are too. They give up something of themselves, as the moon does its light, accepting the little deaths of sacrifice that generate new life. Without them, we, like the moonless earth, would lose our balance completely. Blessed are those who are not self-conscious, for theirs is the Kingdom of Heaven.

Chapter 42

IS IT PRIDE, OR IS IT FEAR?

PEOPLE DON'T TALK about pride much anymore, or even about the capital sins, whose parade was led by pride itself. Pride fell into disfavor from overuse as an explanation for our perversity. It was once the all-purpose vice, the sure diagnosis for every spiritual illness. As observed of the common cold, there was a lot of it going around in the old days.

In a previous era of the spiritual life, pride was the most pursued of vices, just as humility was the most pursued of virtues. There was at times a kind of competition among the devout to dig out pride from the nooks and crannies of the soul where it readily took root. And humility, to think of oneself as nothing, was the wonder drug to kill it off. Now, just as we are wary of the overuse of medication, many believers are afraid they overdid humility in the battle against pride. The self was always under siege and was valued so little that many discovered that they had seriously undermined their own self-confidence. No wonder self-esteem has become the pseudo-virtue of our age, and why there is still so much talk about fulfillment and the development of the individual personality; in part, these are reactions to the long history of highly negative attacks launched against the self to overcome pride.

Pride still lives, of course, and although it has often been described that way it isn't an intellectual vice. For that matter, it isn't even all bad. Pride is more a feeling about ourselves than a way of thinking about ourselves. As such, it is the product of the way we use our personalities in the labor and love of life, not of the way we were but the way we are.

Using ourselves well generates good feeling, a kind of pride that flows from fitting together in relationship to ourselves, to our abilities, and to others. That is a healthy feeling, the feedback akin to the pride of workmanship, the emotional evidence of persons loving themselves rightly. Trying their best, men and women experience a wholesome pride that is quiet and filled with peace.

Pride that is distorted and destructive arises when we operate under false premises about ourselves. This feeling about ourselves is so inflated and pervasive that it edges everybody else out of our lives: it is the invisible energy of a narcissistic age.

Victims of this type of pride do not know themselves and cannot really love themselves sensibly; they can only defend themselves against their own distortions. It is very difficult for such proud persons to love because they would have to break out of themselves to do so. They would rather go down in the loneliness of their self-infatuation than make room for their real selves or for others in their lives. People have been known to be too proud to fight and too proud to beg; the most melancholy of all are those who are too proud to love.

In this extreme form, pride chokes off life as it closes us off from others. The sinfully proud plunder personalities around them, feeding themselves but never really nourishing others. That is narcissism in action. Let a narcissist in your life and you will feel devoured and exhausted. Narcissists use pride as a defense against seeing what they do to themselves and others every day. Such pride runs deeper than our small vanities, such as concerns about the way we look on the outside. That vanity is common and forgivable; the pride that shuts out others is not so common and is always deadly.

The real problem, however, is not the deadly proud persons who nuzzle comfortably into the lining of their own egos. It is, rather, that we have so few people with a healthy sense of pride in themselves, that we have so many characterized not by overconfidence but by underconfidence in themselves. People's lack of self-confidence may be the fruit of all those years of beating the supposed badness of pride out of them. It may be complicated by the pervading sense that so many things in life seem to have gotten beyond our control. In any case, this lack of trust in the self, this nonpride of self-alienation, is an epidemic that outruns narcissism in today's world.

Underconfident persons never get to know themselves very well and never really test their strength in the struggle of life. There is some evidence to suggest that those who never tap their own resources do so out of fear of failure. To avoid the painful consequences of a public setback, they do not involve themselves at all. They shift uneasily on the edges of life, waiting for the right moment when they can step onto the field and no one will laugh at them and no one will criticize them.

They use a perfectionistic defense, always putting off doing this or that until they are sure they have it planned so that they will be immune from criticism. But they never get it perfect enough and so they never get very much done either. Waiting for the moment of no risk at all, these people are always on the sidelines but never really in the game.

The really capital sin is not overbearing pride but this passive and fearful nonparticipation. The mock humility of some of these people covers up their desire to neutralize the conditions of life to keep themselves from ever being in danger. That is to turn away from life altogether. St. Thomas once asked whether it would be better to ask a proud or a fearful person to do something. He answered that he would choose the proud person because then at least something would be done. The fearful one, on the other hand, is overcome by caution and avoids mistakes by avoiding action altogether.

Unfaced fear lies beneath the problems of the persons who cannot trust themselves or take healthy pride in making their best effort, even if that is imperfect. They experience a lot of trouble loving others, too. That is because love subjects us to the biggest risks of all, the danger of being bruised and disappointed by the ones we love. The wounded world needs people who are ready to run some risks, even the risk of being a little proud, for the sake of loving more. A capital sin is committed when the good news of the Gospel goes unpreached because people are too fearful of life to enter into it. Pride won't be the cause of failure as much as the faintheartedness of those who think they are humble when they are really only scared.

Chapter 43

COVETOUSNESS

W E DO NOT CURRENTLY hear the word "covet," certainly not as a sin, perhaps because something like coveting has become a way of life in our consumer culture. For example, the economy would collapse without widespread cultural urges to covet goods of all kinds, useful and unuseful. Covetousness of another's spouse is not uncommon and people act on the impulse all too frequently. "The one with the most toys wins," we are told. But that, as St. Paul says, is to speak of the things of a child that must be put away in the interests of becoming mature.

The problem, of course, is that a case of the covets merely unleashes desires that are usually not very well understood or integrated in the people who experience them. That is why all their longings and all their acquisitions often leave them unhappy, drowning in the deep red sea of debt. Never have so many people owed so much money for unneeded things to so many credit card companies.

And it works the same way for sex. This is a great age for long-distance intimacy and voyeurism for the masses. Entrepreneurs, perspiring freely with erotic enthusiasm, capitalize on the loneliness that lies beneath what we used to call lust by giving humankind a keyhole as big as a movie screen. So we have had an explosion of places called, of all things, "adult" bookstores, movies, books, cassettes, phone exchanges. A recent edition of *Satellite Entertainment Guide* contains nineteen pages of fineprint listings of so-called adult movies and only four columns of religious listings.

These phenomena — more appropriately called adolescent than adult — provide people a place in which they can fan some warmth out of the fires of their own coveting. However, there is nothing more frustrating than the vivid but quickly vanishing fantasies that arouse but never satisfy. That is the trouble with all coveting; it causes anxiety and uneasiness, ravaging rather than satisfying the longing for what rust and moth consume.

You cannot help but look with compassion on people beset with dreams of things and persons beyond their reach. If we have arrived at a new but unnamed emphasis on coveting, we also see that condemning it does not solve the problem. Wisdom bids us to look beneath these longings, to the human spiritual values that give us a center of gravity and a sense of direction in life.

Covetousness — that unruly reaching out for what never fits or brings us happiness — is a human wound that heals only from within. Enlarging people's hearts, helping them to grow to a deeper vision of life and its meaning, letting them know that the Gospels are good news because they tell us how truly to live: these are the right responses for the desolating conflicts that come from too much coveting. Too many churches waste too much breath trying to control the objects of human desires on the outside, condemning books, films, and bad behaviors without helping people put themselves together better on the inside. Covetousness resists the direct attack; it is transformed only as it is absorbed in the spiritual growth process.

Maybe we will deal more effectively with the strangely sown seeds of wanting what we cannot have when we call coveting by its right name again. In this era when even children can speak all the forbidden words out loud, perhaps it is time to speak frankly of the things that cripple us as God's children. Call it covetousness, not bargain-hunting, good economy, a consumer's right to happiness, or virtuous free-market capitalism. For we need something better, something we find not in the marketplace but only in ourselves, by dealing with the spiritual values that never disappoint, grow tarnished, or fail to respond to our deepest longing for an experience of our own lives.

Chapter 44

UNORIGINAL SIN: TABLOID TELEVISION

TABLOID TELEVISION has succeeded on the crystal ball television screen in which we can read, as accurately as ancient seers, what ails us and what we are coming to. By covering the capital sins in action, such programs, according to broadcast analysts, have become immensely popular and extraordinarily profitable. "We cover sex and violence," a host of one of the shows explains, "in varying proportions."

That a new century should begin with the success of such an old formula does tell us something about our lives and why, even as we make fresh resolutions at every New Year, we suspect that we will not keep them very long. It isn't that we sin so greatly. It is more that we seem forever stuck in a No Man's Land between the battle lines of vice and virtue, unable to crawl our way closer to either.

Television's capacity to corrupt us morally has been greatly overstated. The catalog of behaviors directly caused by that staring glass eye in our living rooms is small and not nearly as significant as many observers think. Many people catch diseases from watching the made-for-television films that feature a new and exotic illness every week. Other people apparently learn to drive by observing car chases in crime shows. Worse, yet minor still, many viewers think that sarcastic one-liners are a sign of mature adjustment and the key to happiness in life.

Television is, in fact, a notorious Do-Gooder. Far more than it motivates us to evil, it plies us with advice, cautioning us how to dress for the weather, where to invest our money, what movies to see, and how to avoid traffic jams. A beaming medical doctor warns us on Thanksgiving morning to "eat defensively" at the day's feast, thus spoiling what little fun many men and women get out of their hard-pressed lives.

It is well known that the use of the secret, darkened, and anonymous confessional by sinners seeking personal forgiveness has declined drastically in recent years. Where did all these people go anyway? As it happens, they went on television, eager to confess their most shameful sins, ready to explore the innermost recesses of their hearts in the brightly lit public forum of talk shows. In addition to Helpers' Anonymous, we need Sinners' Anonymous. When members have the urge to confess on television, they call another member up until the urge passes.

So it is not surprising that tabloid television programs, masquerading in the trenchcoats of "investigative journalism," should now be exploring, in their teasing way, murders and adulteries as if they were enlightening instead of just depressing us.

For here, in these jaded programs, we discover why, despite the exhilarating sense that the prospects of a new century bring and the resolutions we may freshly mint, we feel that we are neither making much progress nor slipping far back. This feeling of not getting anywhere, of still being hostage to worries and longings that we cannot eliminate or gratify, is the spiritual dilemma of our age, one of the most salient of all pains of being human.

Tabloid shows play upon the unresolved business of our spiritual growth. They capitalize on fear and desires, the basic problems that we cannot seem to solve or get beyond. As we face life's greatest challenge, to find out and become truly human, we hesitate, largely out of fear or desire, to move forward.

We fear that something will happen to us, that we will put ourselves in peril, or that we will lose everything if we step out of our familiar adjustment. Or we are hampered by desire, some named and others not, for goods or experiences that betray us even as they weigh us down.

The labor organizer Cesar Chavez once spoke to me of the need "to get past the first fear" in order to carry out one's mission in life. That first fear, he said, is "that of losing everything. Once past that, nobody can take anything from you ever again."

Being stuck in the quagmire created by fear and desire is an experience of damnation, which consists in being frozen in that unresolved way-station halfway to who we are and what we could be. We are not free as long as we fail to deal with these basic obstacles to our inner spiritual growth.

The tabloid television programs, something old at a time when we need something new, reflect perfectly the purgatorial condition of American life. Their staple offerings are tales of fear and desire gussied up as violence and sex.

That they should be profitable and popular is not as sensational as it is sad. These programs are actually documentaries of the American soul, running in place, unable to overcome unoriginal sins, those fears and desires that keep it from achieving the truth about itself that would set it free.

Chapter 45

RELIGIOUS MYSTERIES:
WE NEED TIME,
TIME NEEDS US

W E ARE WORKS IN PROGRESS, never finished, and seeds of promise and possibility mature in our souls into the last Shakespearean stage of our lives. The decades of the 1980s and 1990s, research now tells us, are years of flowering more than withering, for growing, creating, and being productive in unexpected ways. We cannot be defined outside this mystery of growth, that great river that, all movement, seems not to move at all.

We do not need crystals, secret words or an initiation ceremony to participate in this moveable feast of religious mystery. We enter this, our human birthright, in standard ways, through believing in, trusting, and loving each other. Yet we cannot draw from the deepest well of our humanity in a hurry.

Simple faith, hope, and love break open the eternal for us but they are experienced and expressed only in the field of time. That is mystery enough in itself, an opening hand at one moment and a closing grasp in the next. Time mentors and monitors our virtues. It demands patience, a willingness to sacrifice minutes and hours we hoard, as misers their gold, for our own uses, to give away our attention, and to defer our own gratification for the sake of others. Prying loose our grasp on itself, time makes lovers of us all.

Such homely virtues are not for the age of the "one night stand," the encounter that by its very name stakes out its time limits like electrified fencing to keep people at a distance after a spurious closeness. It is also accurately referred to as "impersonal sex," because there is no room for being a person — or for meeting another person — within its precincts.

Can time be time if it bars the entrance of humans? Or is it thereby neutered, stripped of its authority, rendered infertile and purgatorial, "wasted" in its deepest sense? Like Dracula with daylight, time turned stale by impersonal inhabitation withers when touched by faith, hope, or real love.

Human growth belongs to a special class of religious mystery that we encounter in time every day. We go to Church or to Temple to have these sightings of mystery ratified and supported, not to find them there. They break time open for us even as they are made accessible only through its portals. This grouping of mystery also includes the pursuit of wisdom, the deepening of love, the development of character, the practice of art, and the experience of healing. These experiences are, in proportionate ways, available to every human being. They demand time, however, the mysterious medium through which we transmit and receive everything worthwhile about ourselves.

Chapter 46

THE AMERICAN DIETER
AND SPIRITUAL MYSTERY

AMERICANS LOVE DIETING so much you would think we would be better at it than we are. Still, we line up, as people once did for patent medicine behind horse-drawn wagons, for the latest pill, theory, or fat substitute that will not only help us lose weight but, according to the pitchman's promise, "keep it off."

Perhaps the homeliest insight of our time — that is, the one whose kernel bears a truth so much bigger than itself that we hate to inspect it — is that dieters who lose weight often gain it back again.

Thus we have the modern reverse version of the myth of Sisyphus, the king of Corinth who was sentenced to push a rock up a hill only to have it roll down every time. Today, we Americans under the same curse toil to erase our poundage from the bathroom scale, only to have it inevitably rebound with a twang of the mechanism's springs that mocks our efforts.

More melancholy, but richly human, are the corollary truths about our appetites and vanities, our good intentions and our questionable rationalizations. Researchers even suggest that we each have a "set point," that is, a destined weight that somehow matches us, a place on the scale which is home to us, a place where we belong and to which we always return.

This idea corresponds with another truth we have come to recognize, that we end up looking the way we should, with the face that, even beneath the counterfeits we try for with cosmetics and surgery, is the authentic signature, the revelation in lines and whorls and pouches of our true selves.

What explains this most common pilgrimage of all Americans? Why do we see people inspecting the packages in supermarkets,

132

mentally calculating the calories, fat, and cholesterol and their potential impact on some imagined ideal of ourselves?

Why, we might ask, has food been gradually deprived of one of its most traditional and valuable functions, to give not only strength but also comfort to people struggling with the basic problem-laden tasks of raising their families, paying their bills, and loving each other?

The answer, perhaps deeper than any provided by the diet zealots who stand as grimly as prison guards on the ramparts of contemporary life, is that the problem is not nutritional but spiritual. In other words, our repetitive struggles to deal with our weight are not fundamentally directed at a physical goal at all. They are instead efforts to achieve something in another realm altogether, the transcendent spiritual order.

Fasting has been recognized all through history as a spiritual exercise. Composed of acts of self-denial, it aims at the mastery of the self, at asserting the powers of the soul over the inclinations of the body.

But fasting has other purposes as well. Holy people, and those so regarded, have employed fasting not only to win spiritual victories over themselves but to win them over other people as well. In his fascinating book *Holy Anorexia,* Rutgers University Professor Rudolph Bell suggests that such great saints as Clare of Assisi and Catherine of Siena employed fasting as a means of asserting their own autonomy in a world that was otherwise dominated by men and a church controlled by male clerics.

These women exercised control in practically the only area in which they were free to do so, carving out a space in which they could stand on their own to preach reform and renewal. In our own day, fasting has been employed by figures as diverse as Gandhi, Dick Gregory, and Cesar Chavez to penetrate and to affect the consciousness and the conscience of their times on behalf of their causes. Fasting was the spiritual instrument of choice in their battles for the freedom of their followers. And food is spiritualized in new stores that claim to sell only natural or "organically grown" food on which no pesticides have ever been sprayed and into which no chemicals have been placed. This is the food, as we have noted, that is immaculately conceived, free of sin, offering a virgin birth in every kitchen in the land.

In such traditional manifestations of fasting we get some clues as to the spiritual rather than the weight problem so many persons are trying to solve through dieting. We also understand why, if losing weight is motivated by something not fully understood or socially appreciated, it will be inconsistent in its effects and results. That is to say, if people don't recognize that their dieting has a spiritual purpose, they will never be truly satisfied with it solely as a physical achievement.

And what is their vexing spiritual dilemma? Americans, living in an environment that seems increasingly beyond their control and in a culture in which those in authority seem so reluctant or unable to use it effectively, are attempting not to live forever but to get some control over the days that they have in the only way that they can. Yearning for authority to re-establish itself sensibly, they are struggling to establish some authority in and over their own lives in the only way they can.

The amount of dieting in America may be a measure, then, not of how overweight we are but of how undernourished and under-instructed we are spiritually. It is a sign of a spiritual destiny we share but do not recognize, a "set point" of the soul that persists in reminding us of our human spiritual identity.

Chapter 47

EVERYDAY MYSTERIES: GETTING TO LOOK THE WAY WE OUGHT TO

A LMOST ALL OF US look cute as infants. But that is about the end of it. Growth allows our imperfection to reassert itself, bringing out the flavor of our uniqueness but, for most of us, our ordinariness as well. Just as we could not be picked out in the nursery, so eventually we cannot be picked out in a crowd, or in a line-up either.

What a melancholy lexicon describes the majority of us for whom comeliness is not destiny when we break out of the chrysalis: average, nondescript, routine, run-of-the-mill, unexceptional, or, hard but durable as a wood floor, plain. Everybody knows who we are at our christening as they ooh and ah over us and call us beautiful, maybe the last time anybody does. Where does all that early promise slip away to?

Our individuality reappears as we grow, awkwardly and not without reverses, into our best selves, in any case, the best we are likely to be. One of the great commonplace religious mysteries is found in our finally getting to look the way we ought to. In our final facial mosaic a well-fitted tile matches every gene; the scars, lines, and wrinkles from living wreathe and merge across the design. Our faces end up as our coat of arms to the world.

We ransom our uniqueness from the faceless crowd by slowly endowing our own features with character. That look of integrity is not an honorary degree but our own lifetime achievement award. We come to look like ourselves the old-fashioned way. We earn it by struggling to become mature, that is, to become ourselves.

Some swim against the tide of getting to look like themselves but they are easy to spot. Like Henry Ford decreeing the Model T, the gods of plastic surgery long ago decided that its practitioners could only reconstruct one model nose and now, like Ford's first automobile for the masses, it is seen everywhere. The popular culture calls it a "nose job," thus unglamorously diminishing the operation and the other great work of surgeons, such as that with burn victims. But the "nose job," certainly literally and perhaps spiritually, diminishes those who receive it. Imagine, for example, implanting the same short straight All-American nose on Mount Rushmore's presidential faces. Such additions become subtractions as they rob our national heroes of the faces they earned through their lives and works.

Because they make them look like everybody else, "nose jobs" make it hard for those who get them ever to look like themselves. Nonetheless, those who choose to alter nature also end up looking the way they should, with the slightly blurred expressions of people unsure of themselves and of who or how they want to be in life. There is a lot of that going around, and it is one of the fiercest pains of being human.

So, too, their slightly puzzled looks represent the legions of men and women who want to do the right thing and end up doing something else. A powerful mystery resides in the associated mystification of men and women bent to the ground under the burden of getting what they thought they really wanted in life.

These are aspects of the religious mystery of revelation, petals from the same process that flowers steadily, although ecclesiastical officials tell us that it ended long ago. Their definition of revelation limits its meaning severely, making it a historical artifact rather than a living experience available to everybody. But religious mystery is essentially a commonplace wonder.

The word is made flesh in every truly human action, even those, such as getting a facelift, that seem remote from the spiritual. Yet every revelation of what we are really like as human beings is rich in insights into the soul. If the pre-Christian philosopher proclaimed that nothing human was foreign to him, believers affirm that nothing human is irreligious to them.

What captures better the glory and pathos of human life than our long journey to our true faces? For now, St. Paul wrote, we know things in a clouded mirror, but in eternity it will be "face to face." Every day, in miniature, we recapitulate the richest of mysteries, that of taking on our own flesh, of bearing its weight and its wounds, of stumbling and rising, of surrendering our lives and finding them again.

Trace elements of mystery are found on all our faces. On them are engraved the truths about faith and hope and love, known and unknown, embraced and unabridged, lost and rediscovered. Where else are there eyes that have peered deeply into the good and the bad of being alive, that have warmed and brightened at the sight of loved ones or been the font of tears for all the sorrows of time?

The Spirit weathers our faces as the wind does the surfaces of canyons and glaciers. This eternal work takes place in and through time, that source of sorrows that is suspended only by love. Then we enter the mystery proper, feeling the eternal in ourselves and in the world. So, even in faces altered by surgery one glimpses all that can be forgiven us humans for our foibles and vanities, for our ambivalence about ourselves and how we want to see and be seen by the world. Is this not something that we all share, something very human, more endearing than anything else, about how we try to put our best face to the world?

Chapter 48

THE REAL MYSTERY
OF TWA 800

R ELIGIOUS MYSTERY is more commonplace than exotic, and is hidden, as all spiritual things are, in plain sight in everyday life. Old railroad stations, John Cheever observed, were built like cathedrals: their vast spaces invited meditation, the sun fell through great windows on marble floors and pew-like benches. Here were celebrated the mysteries of ordinary time: waiting and expectation, separation and reunion, dangerous leavetaking and safe return. This sense of the sacramentality of everyday life hardly survives in airports but our comings and goings, each seeded with mystery, are celebrated every day within them.

The mysteries of TWA Flight 800, broken and consumed above the altar-flat Atlantic on a mid-summer's eve in 1996, have only multiplied and deepened since then. The questions that resist answers are aspects of a mystery greater than how the accident happened or by whose hand, a religious mystery that cannot be solved but only contemplated. In a language softer than that of its tangled debris we hear Flight 800's revelation to us about everything of human importance and meaning.

Against the tell-all code of a shameless television culture, this great ship has held its ultimate secrets to itself, letting go of them in its own time. Some day the reconstruction and analysis of the jet may tell us all the facts. Left will be what radiates gently from Flight 800 even now, the religious mystery in those waters marked forever sacred by the last tongues of flame on its bobbing remains.

Death and Mystery care little for our schedules. Neither of them meets the press or goes on Larry King. Ordinary people must reclaim their own instinct for true mystery, for seeing that the spiritual is not supplied by Special Effects but is part of the fabric of everyday life. Given a chance, average men and women easily recognize the identifying signs of religious mystery.

Perhaps the most distinguishing characteristic of religious mystery is that, Buddha-like, it remains untouched and unmoved by our desires. Silent and majestic as a distant thunderhead, the real mystery of TWA 800 invites us into but does not explain itself to us.

As with the Holocaust, the profoundly holy in our midst transcends our understanding, will not be summed up or settled down, and will never exhaust our meditations or memorials. America, addicted to "talk" as in "talk radio" or "talking about it" in "pseudo-therapy, is stunned by ineffability.

Religious mystery may hide itself but it always reveals the truth about us. As politicians learned in the presence of TWA 800, it is dangerous to squeeze in front of the blinding core of religious mystery. Better than a CAT scan, it lets everybody see right through us.

True religious mystery is more associated with our losses than our gains in life. Spirituality cannot be domesticated into a means for commercial success, à la Dr. Deepak Chopra, without making a sacrilege of its mystery. That is why our personal religious faith, not some abstract dogma, is tested when a mystery as terrible as Flight 800 hovers biblically over the waters.

Traditional faiths, from whose depths the Kaddish and the Dies Irae have been wrenched to give voice to ageless suffering, are cleansed by the flames of tragedy. At such times, ordinary people tell us whether and how real faith works. My cousin Jim Cullen, along with his friend Michael O'Reilly, drew on long-tested belief as he helped pull bodies onto their boat. Listen to him on that darkest of nights as he faced into this grimmest of work: "Mike, they're only bodies. The souls have gone to heaven."

Religious mystery is never a punishment, although that is a favorite theme of some zealots who interpret every tragedy, such as the AIDS epidemic, as God's sword of judgment falling on the unrighteous. Worse still, the New Age cannot address the tragic at all. Death is degraded into an unmentionable enemy, religious mystery becomes cheap grace through crystals, the waters of rebirth come in Evian bottles, and eternal life is confused with living to be a hundred.

Finally, theological mystery always turns our attention back to the ordinary. Flight 800's passenger list was celebrity-free, offering us an uncontaminated sample and the pure revelation of average men and women. Each had already passed what we all dread, a final judgment. Choosing Paris, they responded to what was eternal in their own souls and so passed judgment on themselves by affirming their lives.

In their lives, already full whatever their age, we find a celebration of the everyday virtues that bind life together. Love traveled with Andrew Krukar carrying an engagement ring for his girlfriend. Gharran and Nina Haurani, going to Paris for their twenty-fifth anniversary and Edwin and Ruth Brooks, married fifty-six years, to celebrate her eightieth birthday, paid honor to fidelity.

Hope is found in the young members of the French Club from Montoursville, New Jersey, brimming with curiosity and wonder, with a thirst for knowledge and discovery. David Hogan was returning to Paris to write music while guitarist Marcel Dadi was going home with an award for what he had already played. Before thirty-nine-year-old Jack O'Hara left his top job at ABC sports, he paid tribute to duty by carrying out his last assignment. He had circulated a memo announcing his departure that began, "Change is good."

How much these passengers had accomplished, how much they planned to do on the voyages, so like our own, of going to weddings, celebrating milestones, initiating missions of work, ambition, and simple pleasure. Just like us, we might say, and we thereby pierce the veil of this religious mystery: We hear the voices that sonar cannot sense speaking truths deeper than those that will come out of any investigation. How alive these men and women — our brothers and sisters, our fellow passengers — remain at the heart of this profoundly human religious mystery.

Chapter 49

SCHOLARS AND STARS
SEEK WHAT PLAIN FOLK
NEVER LOST: LOVE

TWO INTERESTING THINGS happened at a recent meeting of the American Anthropological Association. First, at a scientific session on a subject once considered "too mushy" for scheduling, a team of anthropologists reported their surprise at discovering that romantic love, far from being the Western invention it had long been considered, seems to have existed in practically every culture in the world as far back as they could see.

Secondly, the presenters were amazed that the subject of love attracted an overflow crowd, including a "Prime Time Live" television crew. They cried "Eureka!" for finding something that ordinary people had never lost. These supposedly trained observers never noticed that men and women, beneath the get-through-the-day expressions they wear as they are jostled on buses or carried on the tidal flow of crowds, are ever looking or longing for the ones they love. They feel incomplete, as indeed they are, without them. Why, then, were these students of what is human astounded that, whether we register high or low on the scale of sophistication, we are never bored by the subject?

This rediscovery of the wheel of love was publicized on St. Valentine's, that saving day of grace in winter's bleakest bare-treed stretch that transforms frigid urban towers into those of Camelot. St. Valentine's Day is, in fact, blessedly located halfway between the two most overproduced events of the year, the Super Bowl and the Academy Awards.

These spectacles are all artifice and decoration with nothing that lasts at their centers. Love, remembered on Valentine's Day, remains at its core a mystery at once so rich and plain that it challenges both time and death.

The uncertain outcomes of the Super Bowl and the Academy Awards are poor and ineffective substitutes for the mystery in real love. Watching them, however, we exile ourselves from Eden, as, like Adam and Eve, we munch hungrily on the fruit of the Tree of the Knowledge of Good and Evil. It is not an apple through which we lose our innocence; it is Hype. Biting into it, we are seduced to commit unoriginal sins that leave us feeling hungry and depleted every time.

The Super Bowl and the Academy Awards are press agent-intensive, for they are constructed entirely of glitz and expectation. Like marriages made for looks rather than love, they disappoint as soon as they begin and immediately seem as if they will never end. Each must, therefore, be clogged with preliminaries, with massive efforts to prolong the anticipation and to prevent the onion of the actual event from unpeeling its transparent layers too quickly. These can make the Professional Bowlers Tour seem exciting.

That is why, at halftime, people change the channel on the Super Bowl and often go to bed before the last of the interminable Oscars is awarded. Such productions prompt us to additional small unmemorable sins. Under questioning, we deny that we viewed either program, adding, for bad measure, "We don't watch much TV around our place." And then we cannot remember who won last year anyway.

These distracting tent shows, pitched on either side of Valentine's Day, are, despite the barkers and Dixieland bands outside, empty within. They may be a trip but they are not a destination. In contrast, February 14 provides a shelter not for the rich and famous, who often seem unhappy and lonely, but for average people who are not blinded by love but by it are given the vision to see beneath ordinary surfaces to what is wonderful and lovable in each other.

Love seems a torture among the beautiful people who look so perfect on the television and motion picture screens or in the pages of fashion magazines. Yet, among the unsung and the imperfect, it is often filled with magic. That is one of the aspects of the mystery of genuine love that make St. Valentine's Day such an oasis in the desert between such hollow extravaganzas. It is found only between people who are imperfect and who, therefore, must make up for what is lacking in each other. They do that, for example, through being faithful, a transaction that has been often ignored and sometimes ridiculed in the contemporary world. If men and women were perfect, of course, there would be no need for faith, hope, or love, for life would be an error-free environment in which, accompanied by the cold groan of a gigantic computer program, nothing could go wrong.

But, in our human situation, sin, ragged edges, and failure remind us of our unfinished state every day. Acts of belief, hope, and love are not covenants from old treaties or overlawyered clauses in pre-nuptial contracts. They are the living investments of ourselves, exposed at the highest risk of hurt, in other persons. Only through these, each of which has a spiritual cost and a spiritual reward, do we bridge the gaps between us, meeting anew every day halfway across so that we can see each other home again.

When men and women feel these demands and are anxious to meet them, they can be sure that they are in love, just as they can be, as we read in the Cabala of the Jewish tradition, if they feel that in meeting each other that they have found the half of themselves that had been missing previously.

Perhaps some people have trouble finding the half of themselves that is lacking because they want it to resemble the Super Bowl or the Academy Awards. They want to control the outcome the way some teams try to control the ball. Or they want someone else to open an envelope and declare them the winners. That is why, in Chicago, with its tradition of low cunning and love of trapdoors and escapes, a new dating service now arranges for lunches rather than dinner dates between its clients. That just advertises the fear that smothers love before it can take a breath.

Love is not the Super Bowl, thank God, although a ring may well figure into it. Love is a choose-up-sides game among strangers, in which fate seems to join you with others, none of whom is a professional prospect. You have to let yourself go, play for the sake of others, and just forget yourself. That is worth remembering on every Valentine's Day.

Chapter 50

LOVE'S DICTIONARY: THINGS IT ISN'T

A S MANY WAYS as the wind blows, in that many ways and more do we describe love. We might easily get confused by these multiplied contemporary definitions. This is a special problem for the young who are just starting life and who want, more than anything else, to understand and experience love. For many people the test of what anybody says about love is always the Bible, not as a historical book from which all the vitality has been drained by excessive exegesis, but as living words that open us to a loving way of life. Indeed, some of the driest and least appealing definitions of love come from various preachers who study the scriptures more than they experience them. Love that does not have a human face is not love at all.

Some people do give love a bad name. They do not deliberately distort it; it is more a case of their never having known or tasted a love that really held together in their lives or held their lives together. There is no cry sadder than that from people locked outside the meaning of love. For such persons love is always mercurial, slipping away each time they reach for it.

Many search restlessly for love all their lives and the lucky ones are healed by it when they finally find it. But many others keep on searching with a growing and grim knowledge of broken promises, hearts, and relationships, never quite getting hold of the love that they desperately want to believe is still out there waiting somewhere for them.

So intensely do some pursue love that they describe it in battlefield terms. For years the *Chicago Tribune* has run a column called "Tales from the Front" as a forum for those who have been wounded or have found themselves traumatized on the killing fields of human relationships.

Is love, then, something people learn about only the hard way? That is not entirely true, although there is no love free of a full measure of suffering. It is just that it is cruel to mislead people who want and need love with formulas that simply cannot deliver what they promise. There is suffering and struggle enough in the best of love without promoting or permitting any pain to infiltrate it unnecessarily.

But people are desperate for love, and they will, in defiance of their own wisdom and experience, try almost anything to get it. They will, as we know, take advice on love from perfect strangers when they would hardly ever do that about their money. Thus astrologers, soothsayers, psychics, and other assorted prophets of hopeful romance survive and grow rich on the human hope for a touch of love in life.

It is a betrayal of trust to deceive the young (or to agree to their own self-deception) into thinking that they already understand love just because they long for it so. All too often we give them neither the example nor the sense of realism that genuine love demands. There are many voices telling us all, young and old, about love, and it is important to reflect on both what it is and what it isn't.

For example, love is not soft, although it is gentle. There is a big difference. Softness is an undeveloped quality, something that gives way easily because it lacks sufficient structure to hold it together. Gentleness is that wonderful grace-note of strength, something that expresses a person's qualities and character when these have been cleansed free of hurting blemishes. Love is not the powerlessness of a personality too weak to hurt another; it is rather the tenderness of strength monitored and under control.

Love cannot be totally passive, although, especially in New Age musings, some of its definitions are streaked through with this quality. Passivity suggests a shying away from the sharp edges of life and reflects a tendency to look away from, rather than at, the world as it really is. Passivity shrinks back and, in effect, says to life: Respond to me and make me feel loved. But life, in one of the laws of love, says that love does not come to those who are unwilling to love themselves.

This passivity possesses other features worth noting. There is an air of coolness about it, a detachment prized by the people who don't want life to hurt them. Involvement with another person demands something more than the good feelings for which the passive settle. But the code of coolness says that good feelings, the pleasure of another's company, or "having sex together" is possible without really giving of oneself.

We can hold back and protect our emotions and seem to save ourselves from hurt through the strategy of noninvolvement. In this way, people make no claims on each other, pretending that their interaction leaves no permanent traces in life and that they can move back from each other with no harm done. No real investment of the self; no need then to pay the high interest rate of emotional hurt either. They mingle body fluids but they never mingle their souls.

Such self-containment keeps people at a seemingly safe distance from one another but it never leads them to an understanding of love. In fact, this path leads to the emotional desert of loneliness where there are no refreshing oases because there are no people. Only a long and aching loneliness stretches ahead for the cool, the passive, the self open to pleasure while defended against love.

There is an old saying that we can dislike the sin but we must always love the sinner. So too, we may dislike the counterfeit love that is common these days, but we must still love the counterfeit lovers. If we have been blessed enough to know real love in our lives, then we must share it with the people who have lost their way in their search for its meaning. Faith tells us that we can never keep our love just for ourselves, that the infallible sign of the Spirit's presence is love that is given away as freely as it is received. Our task, then, is not to condemn the misguided or the insensitive but to share an accurate vision and experience of love with them.

Chapter 51

INTIMACY AND EMOTIONAL INVOLVEMENT

HALF THE PEOPLE around us speak about the need to get involved while the other half are preoccupied with remaining or getting uninvolved. People long for closeness but, fearing it as they draw closer, they withdraw to the shady preserve of noninvolvement. There coolness acts as an antidote for the heat of emotional involvement that can soar like a fever in close personal relationships. There is not much in life without closeness to others, and there is no closeness without the potential hurts that go with it. There, if ever, we taste "our pain," a suffering specific to humans.

Some people become deliberately involved at every emotional opportunity; others get involved innocently, but their innocence, like that of soldiers in their first battle, is soon erased by the reality of finding themselves close to somebody real.

The young heart is bloodied by first love. Terrible problems go along with caring about other people and what happens to them. This is an inevitable hazard of the initial stirrings of love, an experience so common that almost everyone can still feel the twinges of pain in emotional wounds that they thought had long since healed. How, these people ask, shaking themselves free for the moment from the sleepless nights and the gnawing preoccupations of emotional involvement, can something so good also be so bad?

These reflections describe overinvolvement, of course, and that is the prime danger of any kind of involvement at all. How do we draw the line, or know when things are getting too complex, or when to stay at a slightly restrained distance? When we do not have immediate answers to these deep questions a certain defensiveness of adjustment creeps into our behavior. "I'll never let that happen to me again," we say, remembering still the pain of giving our heart away too freely to someone who, as it turned out, never took us as seriously as we thought. Even first friendships, those tentative probings of the depths of another, generate pain along with wonder. "Keep your distance" is a rule of thumb for emotional survival for those who have been disappointed in friendship or love.

It is hardly a surprise that the model of the so-called professional or objective relationship becomes the option for many. This permits people to stay at a convenient distance from others, with the thermostat of their emotions set at that point where warm blurs into cool. That is a comfortable adjustment because our defense is the pretense that we do not care and never will care enough to let another person hurt us. We can, after all, do without being close to others; we can keep our hearts secure by remaining above it all, never letting a relationship get too warmed up again. How sad the statement of the woman who chose to be childless because, if she had no one to hope in, she would never by disappointed.

And yet no one can really do without others, not for very long anyway. The ability to enter into intimacy with other persons is both the seal and the source of our maturity. This kind of maturity goes beyond although it includes sexual intimacy. It means living and sharing close up to each other, so close that we must be ourselves in relationship to each other or we are really nothing at all. And everything we learn about relationships in psychology reaffirms what the Bible says so often: Sharing what is real about ourselves with others is what gives all the light and warmth to life itself. Psychological jargon has stylized but not really invented the interpersonal realm that describes, as well as anything, what life and real religion are all about. Here we celebrate the whole mystery of being present to each other with as little pretense as possible.

The great wonder of life is that we are not alone, that we can and must make a difference to each other in as personal a way as possible. We are called, each of us, to be friends, not just on good days or when the fancy or our own need strikes us, but on the bleak bad days when even the birds have nothing to sing about. The spiritual life commits us to an active journey, and only love makes us forget the lack of signposts and the long stretches of unpaved roads. The journey is possible only because on it we find not just each other but an understanding of the values of life that we learn only in each other's presence. That is the mystery of intimacy, the lifebase of all true lovers in their growth together in the Spirit.

Love of this kind demands undefended intimacy but, twice shy because of painful involvements, we may decide that the journey of life must be made cautiously and self-protectively. The world does not lack people who settle for arrangements in which they won't be hurt. They are really defending against overinvolvement, giving up because the task of working through the challenge of intimacy seems too much for them. But working through what it means to be in love with another person is what marriage is all about. This is realized, however, only after temporary dizzying fantasies about love wear off or are put aside.

Overinvolvement is an excess of the not yet fully grown, an overinvestment made by those who do not really understand themselves and who may overextend the resources of their personalities before they have consolidated them into a clear identity. There are pains enough in all loving, even for the most mature of us; there is an almost crippling kind of suffering for those who enter a relationship in search of their own identity. Our identity is what we bring to our relationships and, while we will deepen our understanding of ourselves through friendship and love, we court broken hearts if we enter relationships in order to find out who we are.

The first lesson to be learned about intimacy and emotional involvement begins with an examination of our own needs. It is hard to do this, but there is no learning the lessons of involvement if we fail to do so. Very often the biggest hurts, the ones that make us set up the highest defenses, arise precisely because we respond to ourselves more than to other persons. We want them to like us, to respond to us, more than we want to love them. Unless we can get our own needs into focus, we only claw and hurt both our own heart and the hearts of others in the close quarters of friendship and love.

The Spirit touches us when we give as well as take, when we let other people preserve their individuality and preserve our own even in the midst of love. Real involvement means meeting others as they truly are rather than as projections of our own needs and daydreams. When we join what is true in others with what is true in ourselves, then the involvement that is essential to intimacy takes healthy root.

If we do not bring some measure of our own identity and some appreciation of the identity of the other to our relationship, then we are waving a checkered flag or invitation to the suffering we call overinvolvement to race into our lives.

Chapter 52

EVERYTHING HURTS
SOMEBODY SOMETIME

O F ALL THE SIGHS OF LIFE, none is more heartfelt than the one
we breathe when we are emotionally hurt by others. Being
emotionally offended in a profoundly painful experience, so human
and yet so common that everybody knows the feeling firsthand. It
is indeed "our pain," a suffering that links us in the same extended
family.

Most of us put emphasis on the times we have suffered hurt
rather than on the times we have been the cause of it. As long
as we are alive, we sit on the volatile charge of this possibility.
Hurting and being hurt are combustible elements of the human
condition; there is always some danger but, were these necessary
characteristics absent, we would not be human at all.

Some people trade their humanity for insulation from the chance
possibility of being hurt. They close their hatches and plunge far
beneath life's surface, chasing the shadows of the depths to avoid
anyone who seems to them a hunter. They can never get deeply
enough away, however, as their own loneliness, bred of the lack of
light and air and company, reminds them.

As there is something infinitely poignant about their defensive
maneuvers, so, too, there is something wrenchingly sad about their
own testimony about themselves. Nobody's cash was as cold as
that of the late billionaire Jean Paul Getty who, in response to
a question about his many marriages, said, "I've always tried to
avoid being hurt. It doesn't do you any good, letting a woman get
to you that badly. I've been pretty successful at avoiding being hurt,
I think."

You really give up too much of life, no matter how much you
gather in gold, when you try to eliminate hurt from your experience. It is only when we can be touched deeply by another that we

are open enough to life to understand its meaning at all. That is not an easy saying, despite all that is written these days about the risk of real loving. This common hurt is as hard to handle as anything we know. It cannot be ignored and it cannot be laughed off. Sometimes, because of circumstances, there is nothing we can do but feel the pain of it, the throbbing throughout our person that won't go away no matter how we try to distract ourselves.

This happens when we are hurt by the person we love most, the one to whom we usually come when emotionally wounded and misunderstood by others. There is no hurt like this one. This misunderstanding, no matter how momentary, cuts so deeply that we cannot even speak without making it hurt more. It is the hurt that makes us back away from each other, from those we trust and hold most dear, as if some cruel fate has suddenly made us into strangers again. Time brings things back into focus, but there are no moments lonelier than those when hurt comes from the ones we love.

The reason for this is clear enough, whether it happens between husband and wife, old friends, or young lovers looking forward to a life together. When they are real, love and trust enable us to lower our guard and open our real selves to others; we are most vulnerable to our beloved, most defenseless with those we really love most. That is why when something goes wrong the pain is so intense. We do not have any defenses up, nothing to shield us from the blow, no matter how unintentionally it is delivered. We feel its full force and hear the very breath that it knocks out of us at the same time. In moments of such hurt, misunderstanding cuts through our innards like a hot blade.

At times like these, times we try to avoid as much as possible, we might think of the fact that this is how the persons we love feel when, however unintentionally, we hurt them. Knowing the sting of such hurt, we may become more careful not to inflict this kind of suffering on others. Random thoughtlessness is a big element in some of the deepest hurts of life. Nobody really means to hurt the other, especially when the other is near and dear, and yet we go right on doing it all the time. There are all kinds of cuts, kind and unkind, that we give others without really noticing it. We must work hard for the maturity that attunes us to what a deadly weapon our own thoughtlessness can be.

There is recurring speculation about how we all share some corporate or national guilt for this or that event, for historical and cultural problems of all kinds. It is really much easier to make that kind of global accusation against ourselves than to face the real injuries we do one by one and quite personally to one another. The latter is hard because we know the searing quality of hurt, and it is not pleasant to think that we can inflict it on others. Some of us even like to feel sorry for ourselves and nurse our hurts as long as we can. That is why, I think, Christ made so much of wholehearted forgiveness.

There would be no healing for us at all unless we could grant each other real forgiveness. That is not easy because, once we are hurt, we are likely to keep our guard up for a while afterward. But real forgiveness, the profoundly spiritual element that restores wholeness to people, is given only if we are willing to drop our guard once more. Forgiveness demands that we make ourselves open to getting hurt all over again. You cannot settle out of court, with neither party admitting blame.

Forgiving asks more from us than a quick mea culpa or an embarrassed wish that both we and the injured party would forget that this or that has happened. Forgiveness comes from people who have hurt each other but are willing, out of the love that gives them that awful power still, to run the risk that it may happen again. That is the only remedy there is for the hurts we give to one another.

The scar tissue on lovers' hearts is the sign of the two-edged power of love itself. It is only because love makes us so open and trusting that it also makes us targets for each other's occasional insensitivity. Through the power of that same love, a spiritual gift, we can bring our faith in each other to even greater fullness. That faith makes human beings whole. Love is what holds our lives together and strengthens us for the perils of the life in which everybody hurts somebody sometime. We are all responsible for seeing that the human family, full of hurts and aches, experiences more of the loving forgiveness that is written about in the Gospels.

Chapter 53

LOVE'S MOMENT REMEMBERED

LOVE LASTS, St. Paul and our own experience tell us, but we never take this truth as seriously as we should. Love endures, carries on its effects in us, and continues to be powerful well beyond the moment or the relationship in which it is experienced.

Love is not like food that provides temporary nourishment but does not permanently stay the rhythm of hunger. Love gives us abiding strength because it adds something to us that does not ebb away of itself. It is seed and flower of human growth and there is no going back on growth that has been achieved.

Love that we have really known from another lives on in us even when the other leaves us through death or separation. It is the fire burning brightly inside us, lighting our way and warming us for the days when we are alone or under stress. It kindles our own motivation and our own power to love; we can give love away every day without losing any of it.

Thinking about love in very limited ways we are too intimidated by the songs and stories that mourn or fear its loss. We lessen our chances of experiencing love when we are dominated by the fear of its slipping out of our grasp.

That is not the way of real love, which is made of far more durable material. It is, however, the way of the many inadequate and substitute notions of love that fill popular culture. That is the love we try to demand of another as an account payable, or the wish of love that is merely a passing attraction, an erotic imperative or the echo of our own need.

A great mystery suffuses real love and it has never been fully captured by poets, artists, or sentimental preachers. Solid and deep, it constitutes a miracle far more common than visions or wonders, for it is a wonder in itself that cannot be bartered or put safely away like gold, in some chill private vault of our personality. Love does not seek a hiding place; it demands sunshine and fresh air and never tires of singing of itself to others.

Genuine love is active, its dynamism undiminished by the passing of years or the shifting of circumstances. Of its essence, such love is creative; it generates and sustains life. It craves being out in the open where it can grow and spread to others.

Believers, least of all, can view love as a perishable commodity, or as something that must be locked away from life itself. And the most unacceptable notion of all, if we take the Bible seriously, is that love is destructive. It is powerful, yes, but it is not destructive. It flourishes in those who face unafraid and undefended the problems of loving and the hurts that life regularly inflicts. The real danger exists for those who never want to face these things and who can never, therefore, experience any real love at all.

It is strange that so many believers remain shy about loving and seem so unwilling to open themselves to it or to let others open themselves to it. They choose rather to build walls and fences against the supposed dangers of love, and so they never know the moment of love or its continuing power. Lonely are those who do not let themselves understand that real love casts out the haunting stalker of all life, fear.

The mystery in love breaks down walls and topples over fences. It does not confine itself to one relationship or one style of relationship. Love is found in many places and we would not be afraid of it if we really believed in its spiritual power. Any love that is selfless is the work of the Spirit, the action of God in our lives, the evidence we can know that supports our faith and our hope. Because it is the sign of God touching our lives, it is powerful and creative. As Robert Johann has written, those who love are given a "glimpse of the world beyond care."

The most distinguishing mark of lasting and creative love is found in its intrinsic sense of responsibility. This is far different from the hit-and-run tactics of those who use other people for a while and then put them aside. It is a world away from those who only play at loving others with glowing phrases but who use their mastery of the manipulative arts to use the other and move on.

Love is meant to last, and so it imposes a telling discipline of its own, a discipline that flows from a sense of being responsible for the other in season and out. Real loves are committed to the good of the other and not just to the satisfaction of their own need. A genuine lover wants the beloved to grow; only the counterfeit lover wants to control the other in all the aspects of life.

The lessons of loving are not mastered all at once. They require a lifetime of learning. Perhaps in the human condition we must settle for getting better at it as the years go by. Understanding this truth is one of the effects of real love; it matches the way men and women are and helps them to continue the process of growing out of themselves. That is why love lasts and enables us to learn to share it even with our enemies. The scriptures tells us all of this, just as they tell us that it is never too late to respond to the Spirit of love that can so transform our lives.

It is often the remembered moments of love that keep us going beyond what seems to be the last outpost of our own strength. When love is real it makes a powerful mark on us, enlarging us and moving us always forward. Love's inherent authority makes it more powerful than death or any of the dangers of life itself. Love is what believers should be good at so that, observing them, the whole world can be strengthened and can learn to put away its fears.

Humans always want to leave something lasting behind themselves. Only the mighty or the highly gifted have the chance to do this through history, the arts, or endowed buildings. All persons, however, leave something that outlasts the greatest fame or accomplishment when they reach out, even for a few moments, to love somebody else. That reaching out — so precarious and yet so transforming — is the essential movement of love wherever it is found.

We touch the ways and destinies of every fellow human when we love another with deep responsibility. We become instruments of life, ever-increasing life, when we truly love. Our names may be forgotten but our presence survives in the love that is the only thing we can really leave behind us.

Chapter 54

THE WORK OF LOVE

E VERYBODY HAS HEARD Sigmund Freud's famous answer to the question about our purpose in life. "To love and to work," he said, a reply at once profound and simple. It may seem strange to associate love and work, especially to a generation whose romantic expectations run so very high. Love, however, is work, and hard work at that. It disintegrates quickly in the lives of those who do not understand this.

Love is not work in the way that digging ditches is. It would, in fact, be less exhausting if it were something quite so routine and predictable. We can dig ditches and think of something else at the same time. We cannot, however, love another person and have our minds and hearts on something else at the same time.

We may speak loving words, or send candy and flowers, but if our person is not really involved in a committed and consistent way, the whole thing is fake and falls apart quickly. Few things demand as much constant attention and willing effort to be fully present to another as love. Love is filled with wonder and warmth and the world moving under our feet; it also demands concentration and the hard work of staying in relationship to another through all the problems and difficulties of life.

It is natural, of course, for people not to talk much about the discipline involved in loving another person responsibly. We like the bright sides of things, and love is no exception. It is a terrible predicament, however, for an individual to long for love and yet to shrink back from the hard work that is its unpublicized but full reality. The hard work is as simple as the effort that goes into knowing and really accepting others once their eccentricities are exposed under the harsh light of close living. Love's labor is involved in persevering at the effort to understand others even after we think we have heard everything they have to say.

The work of love is hard indeed when it demands that we over-

156

come our tendency to turn inside ourselves when we are hurt. It is hard work to try to be vital and responsive to others when we are tired and would just as soon be left alone. Love is very demanding of the best of our energies in moments of tension and misunderstanding with those we love. We are tempted to let all that is hostile bubble up at those moments, to feel we have a right to a primal scream; it is hard work to face our anger and to keep it from destroying our love.

You don't hear much about this side of love. In fact, you hear more about people who give up on trying to work out their lives together. How many love songs are written in the past tense! Some people pass up too many chances to take the risk of love and its demands; others are overwhelmed by the day in, day out challenges of faithful loving. They want what can never be, that love be easy, that it be given to them rather than be demanded of them, and so they are unprepared for its reality. They do not even understand that embracing the painful work of loving makes it secure and solid; they do not grasp that in suffering the death love asks of us we find rather than lose our lives.

One is struck, for example, by the tender reflections of the late South African author Alan Paton in *For You Departed*, the memoir he addressed to his late wife. He wrote with the simple openness of a man who had to face the hard work and suffering of very deep love. Paton had married a young widow who continued to wear her first wedding ring. When they had been married for some time he experienced a strong attraction to a young woman student of his. Addressing his wife in retrospect, Paton wrote:

You suddenly said to me, Are you in love with Joan? And I said, Yes. You said, What are you going to do about it? and I said, Stop it. You said, Surely, she must be consulted about it, and I said, We have already spoken about it. Then I said to you, I ask only one thing and that is to go down to Natal and say goodbye to her, to which you replied, I am willing that you should. Later that day, or that night, you said to me, What did I do wrong? But I cannot remember what I answered, or if I answered at all.

Paton went to see the girl, ended their relationship, and returned home:

You met me at the door of the house, and you took me into your arms in that fierce way of yours, and you held back your head so that I could see the earnestness in your face, and you said to me, I am going to make it all up to you. I do not know when I noticed that you were no longer wearing your first wedding ring, but that night when we went to bed it had gone from your finger. All I know is that when you died I searched the house for it. Strange, is it not, that if I found it I would have treasured it? It is a strange story altogether, isn't it? But it is a true story of life, and if I lived it again I'd like to live it the same way, only better.

This kind of facing a complicated truth together is by no means easy. Without a generous willingness born of faith in each other to work at their love the story could have gone quite differently. Similar, if less dramatic, challenges fill the calendar of every married life, of every friendship, too. Love that isn't ready to work hard at patient sharing and understanding doesn't survive such crises. Remember the advice of Ann Landers: "Marriages may be made in heaven, but the maintenance work is done down here on earth."

For believers these crises are occasions for the growth together that the Spirit gives those who willingly join themselves to the struggles and labors of love. Through the work of love men and women discover its real meaning. Embracing that, they redeem each other.

Chapter 55

THE BITTERSWEET ADVENTURE: LEARNING TO LOVE

FEW EXPERIENCES are more damaging to a person's psyche than finding the love they thought real first cracking ominously and then disintegrating completely on them. Such shocks come mostly to people who are just learning how to love. This vulnerability goes along with getting close to somebody else in both friendship and love, but it is most prevalent, sometimes epidemic, during adolescence, whenever that may come.

This pitfall of growing is a danger to anyone opening up for the first time to the magic of discovering the wonders of someone else. Sometimes this experience must take place in friendship before it can take place in love. Important lessons are learned as we move out of ourselves and toward other people in our first great adventure of friendship. During this expanding period of our lives we first sense the mysterious blend of idealism and deepened self-consciousness that accompanies our being born again by breaking out of our shells, drawn by the magnet of the other.

The German author Thomas Mann catches an aspect of this experience in his famous story Tonio Kroger. It opens with Tonio waiting after school for his friend Hans; they had agreed to go for a walk together. Tonio is deeply wounded when he notices that Hans had almost forgotten their engagement. He forgives Hans, however, when he sees his friend's remorse. But they still feel this near-misunderstanding as they start their walk:

> Tonio did not speak. He suffered. His rather oblique brows were drawn together in a frown, his lips were rounded to a whistle, he gazed into space with his head on one side. Posture and manner were habitual.
>
> Suddenly Hans shoved his arm into Tonio's, with a sideways look — he knew very well what the trouble was. And

Tonio, though he was silent for the next few steps, felt his heart soften.

"I hadn't forgotten, you see, Tonio," Hans said, gazing at the pavement. "I only thought it wouldn't come off today because it was so wet and windy. But I don't mind that at all, and it's jolly of you to have waited. I thought you had gone home, and I was cross. . . . "

The truth was, Tonio loved Hans Hansen, and had already suffered much on his account. He who loves the more is the inferior and must suffer; in this hard and simple fact this fourteen-year-old soul had already been instructed by life.*

The same poignant quality edges all the experience of young love and new friendship. But we learn a great deal about ourselves through these encounters; indeed, we cannot grow up without them. They make us vulnerable, however, to the special hurts and misunderstandings that sweep our hearts as plagues do weakened populations when we are not sure of our relationship with someone whose affection we prize. In fact, we all suffer precisely because there is so much self-concern and self-need involved in this kind of developing love.

We do not know it, and we cannot really admit it, but these relationships are just the beginnings of love — the first wrenching away from our own inner world. Nor is it surprising that these first lessons in learning how to love should be filled with so many mistakes. That is what happens when we try to learn anything, and we should not be amazed to see faults, jealousies, and other miscalculations of the heart filling the space known as first love. This experience is to be expected rather than unexpected at that time of life when people are beginning to reach out to each other.

People do hurt each other — even as they misunderstand each other — in more serious ways than by forgetting about a plan to walk home from school together. Unfortunately, this period of exploration and discovery lacks many sure guides, despite the fact that we know of the hazardous reefs and landfalls that mark its course. In other words, we must let young people learn to love the hard way, by letting them set off on the painful path of misunderstanding and allow them to make mistakes as they learn to climb

---

Stories of Three Decades (New York: Alfred A. Knopf, 1936).

out of their own egos and make room for someone who is truly different from — rather than just an extension of — themselves.

When we understand that first loves are not usually final loves and that what is learned is far greater in the long run than what is lost, we may be able to sit with young persons whose love has just ended and sympathize with a deep and lifegiving understanding. Failures in the beginnings of love do not end everything; such persons have, in fact, taken a big step toward a greater capacity for love because the experience rolls away the stone on the entrance to their hearts. We help best if we refrain from giving any final answers and try not to close wounds quickly that must heal slowly from the inside.

We must stick with brokenhearted lovers at such moments, not mocking them or falsely reassuring them. If we make ourselves present and convey that we understand because we have had a similar experience in our lives, we help keep young hearts open to the love that will come in richer, more mature, and more lasting form. What we do, in other words, is help them learn something new about themselves and about life. And to help others learn solidly about the love that still lies ahead is a very great thing indeed.

Chapter 56

ANOTHER KIND OF LOVE: LEAVING PEOPLE ALONE

THE CATALOGUE OF MISFORTUNES we humans inflict on each other in the name of love is large indeed. Throughout the course of history people have done the most astounding things to each other, always with the energetic reassurance that the sole motive for the action is love. This begins early with large spoonfuls of bitter medicine held firmly in reportedly loving parental hands; doctors and dentists lulling us into an innocent vulnerability with promises that "this won't hurt a bit"; the father of the family administering some heavy-handed discipline to a soft-bottomed child with the unlikely protest that "this hurts me more than you."

It is a part of wisdom to understand that people who love each other must allow each other to suffer at times. Life must be faced and the pain is made tolerable only because someone else does love us and supports us through it, even when he or she cannot prevent it.

This understanding is found between husbands and wives, and between them and their children; friends know this experience as well. It is not easy to let someone you love suffer a crisis of growth, an illness, or a trying experience at school or at work. But lovers face these things all the time and redeem each other through entering into them together.

Far different from this, and distinctly nonredemptive, are the people who move into the lives of others with plans for remodeling them. Like amateurs who try to remodel anything, they are confused about their purpose, their motivation, and their skills. They frequently end up causing a good deal of damage.

This is the case with meddlers who operate under the banner of love as they charge into the inner precincts of another person's personality. They call this destructive foray by the name of love, manifesting this understanding of love in a wide variety of situations. You see it in the busybody who has plans for remodeling you and is always willing to share them with you. We are surrounded by people with such "loving" plans.

Other needy people want you to respond emotionally to them and manipulate you, even to the quoting of scripture, to get you to do so. Familiar as well are the enthusiasts for some particular form of prayer or alleged spiritual experience who absolutely insist that you join them. Worst of all, I suppose, are individuals who insert themselves into the relationship of two other people with the supreme self-confidence that their loving intervention will help the others to function better in some way or other. Perhaps they have had a hand in making America into a land of victims.

The M.O. of meddlers can be easily recognized: First of all, they are hopelessly insensitive to themselves and to other people. Most prominent is the central role their own needs play in their forging relationships with others. They do not seek the good of the other nearly as much as the satisfaction of some drive or need of their own. They do not admit this, of course, and cover it by invoking the notion of love. Because of their superficial understanding of it they give love a bad name.

The core difference between such victimizers and true lovers lies in the self-centeredness of the former and the selflessness of the latter. Real lovers put themselves and their own needs to death for your sake; real meddlers smother you to death for their own sake. Lovers, even when they are leaving you to your own pain, prize you; victimizers, even as they interfere with your life, prize themselves way ahead of anyone else.

Real love, as Paul wrote to the Corinthians, is very understanding. It does not seek itself. Perhaps St. Paul could just as well have written that real love knows when to leave other people alone.

Chapter 57

FAITHFULNESS

THE PRESENT CLIMATE of our country offers little encouragement for the faithful person. Indeed, persons who try to keep their commitments as best they can must get discouraged when they see infidelity ignored, exalted, excused, or rewarded. Nonheroes, adulterers, deserters — the dying century has praised them all of late. The real question must be: Why is anybody faithful in a popular culture that fails to recognize or support it?

It is not easy to remain faithful to our spouses, our responsibilities, our convictions or our word, when the world makes it easy for us to put them aside. An affair outside marriage, some people continue to say, is good for the marriage, or at least good for you, and not necessarily harmful to the marriage, especially if the other partner does not know about it. Tolerance of infidelity turns into praise or ironic acceptance in this morally dulled period. "No-fault" divorce helped adultery to disappear even as a legal entity a generation and more ago. Even the president of the country flaunts his freewheeling sexual morality: How could the average person struggling to be faithful feel except discouraged and alienated?

Much of the glorification of extramarital adventures comes from clever but superficial minds. Advocates of the "good life" never have to pay the price for the kind of behavior that they encourage in others. Neither do other social observers or moralists who, on frequently shaky kinds of data, find good or at least "neutral" things in unfaithfulness, broken promises, or broken families. They are removed from the anguish of everyday life, and they seem at times quite insensitive to the widespread signs of our longing for some affirmation of faithfulness.

The latter comes across, among other places, in the women's magazines where hardly an issue appears that does not contain one of more articles expressing a woman's uneasiness about the faithfulness of spouses in marriage. It comes across in the cries of youth who are searching, as much as for anything else, for some adults in whom they can truly believe. It is hard for them to trust people whose behavior seems to them to be marked by too many sellouts to forms of infidelity.

It is striking that the world has so little to say that is positive about the concept of faithfulness. Perhaps it has lost hope because it has known so much of disappointment. It is surely here that believers have something to say and something to show to the world. If, as psychiatrist Leon Salzman noted in his extensive research on infidelity, there is always some failure of commitment, some lack of real love involved, it is clearly a religious obligation and a spiritual work to offer a better understanding of these things to the world. Underneath all the glorification and pseudo-sophistication, infidelity flourishes where people forget how to love each other and give up the sometimes difficult work of staying in love with one another.

Believers who try to live by the spiritual principles offer the world some insight into what is demanded of those who would spend a lifetime together. Love, when it is understood as a process of growth that includes joys and pains, is a distinct challenge to the concepts of instant gratification and "Let's not make any claims on each other" that are so often presented as if they were natural truths.

The most revolutionary thing a believer can stand for is not a bloody uprising against some "establishment" but a real belief in the meaning of love. That is not easy because it demands that men and women continue their search of themselves and of each other, that they continue to listen and to grow in relationship with each other, even as age and circumstances work great changes in them.

It is getting easier all the time to give up when a relationship finds itself in difficulty. People who buy this philosophy gradually find that there is no center of gravity in their lives, that their identity is a smear, and that their restlessness is not quieted by all the mood music culture plays to practice infidelity by.

If Salzman's assessment of his clinical experience is correct, then it is more important than ever to preach the spiritual message to others. Perhaps believers need a few words of encouragement that they are on the right track when they continue to believe and trust and suffer through things with each other. Our greatest infidelity is that lack of faith in the world we profess when we lose confidence in the saving power of keeping faith with each other in cynical times.

Chapter 58

ISN'T LOVE DANGEROUS?

T HAT IS THE GIST of many questions I have been asked at lectures, through the mail, and even from fellow airplane passengers. The question is usually couched in words that reveal longing and uneasiness; it comes out of the hearts of people who want to be part of real life but who also want to be careful and do the right thing.

There is, in fact, nothing more powerful and therefore nothing more dangerous than love. So it has been throughout history. Yet, though there is nothing more dangerous than love, there is nothing so essential to life either. This is a danger with which we must live if we seriously intend to enter and inhabit our lives fully. Thus we face the inevitability of love's entrance into the hearts of all who open themselves to others.

More dangerous even than love, however, is the possibility of a life without love, of an existence that, purged of affection and tenderness, is a "proper" kind of life armored against passion or caring. The biggest threat to humanity is living a chilly shadowed life because we fear the sunshine of sharing with others. Love seems especially dangerous for those who so fear its complications that they defend themselves against even the possibility of letting others draw close to them. When we are afraid, everything looks dangerous to us.

Yes, love is dangerous; it always has been, and evidently it always will be. But it is also a wonderful enlarging of the self and, in the long run, the only emotion in which we can place our hope. So, live dangerously; it beats not living at all.

Chapter 59

DO YOU EVER FEEL
YOU HAVE RUN OUT OF FAITH?

"F AITH," a reflective friend once said, "is what you run out of in life." He put into words a feeling that all of us know well. There are times when things pile up and our spirits sag, dark hours when we wonder if our strength has not been mined out at last. We have been running the race, we would like to finish the course, but can we possibly keep the faith?

Faith under stress does not immediately refer to our willingness to accept this or that particular formulation of dogmatic teaching. That is easy compared to something more fundamental, something deep in our being, our very capacity for any kind of belief at all.

This resides in the core of personality, the ground of our relationship to God, ourselves, and each other. Suddenly eroded and uncertain, its terrain illuminated by lightning flashes of weariness or disappointment, it can seem too terrible to travel further across it. We feel almost overwhelmed, struck numb by doubts about our own or God's power to help. This desperate feeling causes us to experience great loneliness. Life looms up as an underestimated challenge that neither asks or grants ground, that presses us just as we are running out of physical and spiritual energy.

There are many faces to this assault on our faith. A husband and wife wonder at times whether they can keep on believing in one another, whether they can continue to respond to one another for better or for worse. They need faith in each other and in God precisely at moments when they seem to have the least amount of it left.

There is something absolute in the act of trust they must make at such times; absolute, because all other emotions seem drained away; absolute, because if they cannot count on each other they can count on nothing at all; absolute, because it is all or nothing.

Their sighs tell us how much they feel the burden of each other. The honeymoon is long past and nothing is certain about the future. Strength seems to come only from moment to moment, and understanding is hard to generate. They know everything that is wrong with each of them.

But somehow, in facing this experience fully together they communicate what they could never say in words to one another. They share a desperate moment as deeply as they have shared more happy times. The important thing is that they really share something, even when there seems precious little left to share.

Their anguish is not different from that of parents who know they must believe in their children if they are to help them to grow but who find the steady investment of their care and attention increasingly difficult to make. What world have they made for their children, and how can they blend trust and concern in such a way that the child is neither abandoned nor overprotected? What can they believe in when a child becomes ill or dies? Their churches may seem unsteady, caught up in conflicts of their own, absorbed with institutional problems, and so sources of concern as much as sources of support. Such parents cannot help wondering about the sacrifices they made for their faith with such confidence at an earlier time.

All these situations are painful because nobody speaks any magical or soothing words. There is just life, at once powerful and fragile, to be faced and borne with whatever reserves one has left. The experience is so common in our day that we might weep for recognizing each other in it. At these bleak far ends of life we find and can redeem each other. It is not that one of the other of us has all the answers to clear away the doubts. Nor can some charismatic figure provide a previously untried spiritual nostrum to invigorate us.

Redeeming trust is found, as it is for husband and wife, in opening ourselves even a little bit to each other. We thereby get the strength that comes from sharing something very real about life. We are truly in touch with each other and that is an increasingly rare experience in the great, slick pop culture that tends to make us competitors rather than friends or just lonely strangers on the same crowded bus together. Our culture specializes in surfaces, whether these are television screens, high fashion, or the smoothly styled shells of automobiles. It markets allegiances, whether to baseball teams or brand names, but it does not provide much in the way of sustaining faith. This comes only from experiences in depth, and they are found only between human beings.

Sustaining faith is our free gift to each other. If we do not share enough of life at the times when we feel sure of ourselves, we can find something real to share at those moments when our faith is weak, even if it is only our own emptiness. We are more truly ourselves when our confidence is shaken for it strips away pretense. We are more open to each other and also to the Spirit. Maybe it works because we are so genuine, so appealingly human, so much in need of each other at these times.

Such times occur every day. We need the rebirth of faith that comes from the response of other humans. "How can I believe" — the old question is as fresh as ever — "unless some man shows me?" The renewal of ourselves, the restoration of our trust, is ever and always mediated by our relationships with other humans. Faith doesn't fall from the skies; it comes to life in our human experience. Churches and temples exist only to recognize and underscore this, to remind us and reinforce this fundamental spiritual truth.

It is interesting to note that when St. Paul wanted to strengthen the faith of his fledgling communities, he reminded them of their obligations to help each other in a very personal way. You have heard the good news, he says over and over again, and now you must share life together.

"You should carry each other's troubles," he writes to the Galatians as he might to us, "and fulfill the law of Christ." And to the Ephesians just as clearly, "Be friends with one another, and kind, forgiving each other as readily as God forgave you in Christ."

The measure of our faith, and the sign of our participation in the mystery of the Redemption, is our willingness to reach out to one another even at the price of letting our own weakness be revealed in the process. The fundamental trust involved in this self-revelation builds our own and our neighbor's strength.

God chooses the weak things of the world because that is the way that most of us are; we can glory in this weakness because it makes room for the action of the Spirit. The tensions of life become unbearable only when we sentence each other to suffer them alone.

Chapter 60

JUST WHOM DO WE TRUST?

THE WORD "trust" is now associated as much with economics as with human relationships, as, for example, in irrevocable trusts that, once set up, cannot be altered. Trust is better known, of course, as one of the basic ingredients of life. We do not grow unless we receive it freely from others and we are not grown unless we can give it away freely to others. Trust is an awesome and difficult aspect of life, and a dangerous one too.

Unlike the special economic species, all human trust is revocable. It is not a fixed or unchanging entity any more than life itself is. It can be taken back, it can be lost, or it can be given anew. Trust is alive and cannot be thought of as fixed or static. Trust means something only when it costs something to give it. It transforms people's lives when it is freely given without question or condition by those who are not afraid of the dangers of such generosity.

Trust is the quality that warms the environment of the young, expanding their opportunities to grow and to find themselves and the way that is right for them in life. In trust we see a flash of the ineffable magic that shines in the lives of people who really love each other. When they trust each other they are open and undefended, totally present to each other and, as a consequence, totally vulnerable to the hurts they may, in greater or lesser ways, inflict on each other.

Trust is that extraordinary quality by which we make room in our lives for other people, letting them see what we are really like. It is the kind of largeness of heart and spirit that allows us to view others as separate from ourselves and in need of the special freedom that trusting people grant to each other. Trust is the touch of the Spirit that casts out fear and makes it safe for other people to be themselves freely in our presence and in life beyond.

We are always looking for someone we can really trust. Philosopher Richard Rorty writes that we must settle for irony because nothing better is possible, certainly not truth. Yet all around us people still seem able to pay the price of actively trusting one another. Not trusting shields the human heart from hurt. It is dangerous indeed to expose our emotions to the very special pain of abused trust. The fear of being hurt is almost an epidemic disease and so people substitute bulletproof vests of defensiveness, for irony, for example. But irony does not cast out fear; it doesn't even keep it at bay very long or very well.

Defensive people never feel very secure, and when they withhold trust, whether in family matters or in business, they accelerate uneasiness and mistrust all around themselves. Only love casts out that kind of fear, love of which trust is an essential component. It takes a lot of growing to give ourselves away in trust, all the while running the risk of being betrayed; it is as hard as anything we are ever likely to know: to love others enough to let them be separate rather than to control them, to be trusting even after we have been hurt. This trust cannot be given half-heartedly or in installments. We give all of it, all at once, or it lacks the authority that generates growth in others.

Trust has many faces. It can be as simple as giving our attention to a troubled person when we would rather be doing something else. Withholding that commitment of our energies and interest we present only a semblance of ourselves, just enough to look interested but not enough to be touched or involved or to be hurt. Full-bodied trust is an easy thing to talk about but a hard thing to give. There is no unspoken sentiment more common than "I trust you but I'll keep an eye on you."

Many parents claim to trust their children. What they sometimes mean is that they let the children do whatever they feel like. They then pull back into their own lives because the work of trusting is too much for them. Here we come upon a fork in the road of trust. Persons who really trust others offer them support and stick with them. They do not reassure them and then back away defensively. Because the emotional abandonment of others is all too common, trust is sometimes very hard to find. It is so much simpler to offer the campaign-promise kind of trust — the kind that solicits a vote of confidence that enhances us but that we never deliver afterward.

Nor can trust ever be successfully pretended. It is not a function of "presentation," "image making," or "perception." People immediately see through the shallow and superficial pseudo-trust that cuts off rather than encourages involvement with others. This is by no means restricted only to parents.

You may witness it at times in the very young who talk a good deal about trusting each other. Underneath it all, they are really saying, "Let's not demand anything of each other. Let's not take away each other's freedom." This only sounds like trust but the anxiety about not making demands tells us quickly that it is by no means the real thing.

We can tell when we are trusted and so we should recognize when we are challenged to trust others. Trust does take away some of our freedom and limits our choices. Trust keeps asking something from us long after the moment passes in which we give it to someone else. Trust's hallmark is the continuing concern and support we offer to others by keeping ourselves both available and vulnerable to them.

Trust is an ongoing process rather than a one-time payment. It is not a yellowed document hidden in a safe-deposit box, nor an exchange of vows that grows weaker as we grow older. Trusting people is a spiritual way of living with them on a long-term basis. Those who trust are genuinely rich in the things of the Spirit, because the more they give trust away, the more they receive and the deeper their lives become.

Chapter 61

FINDING THE CENTER
OF THE UNIVERSE

NOT MUCH GOOD is said about people these days. Murphy's law that "anything that can go wrong will go wrong" prevails. The human race is under multiple indictments, and nobody even seems interested in making bail money for it. Add self-inflicted wounds and the penchant for pleading guilty to every charge, and one begins to understand this abused condition.

It is small wonder that those who really want to lead decent, loving, and law-abiding lives are discouraged. They have been accused of bulldozing down the past whose traditions they do not respect, polluting the present whose problems they do not understand, and destroying the future whose promise they do not foresee. Modern persons have shot down and stuffed the dove of peace, bartered away their sexual maturity for a mess of erotic pottage, and sacrificed their freedom to the gods of technology. Quite hung up, they have sold out, been taken in, and have little heart to break through. They constitute, it would seem, the hazardous waste of history.

Those who feel that the year 2000 is the lid on a Pandora's box forget that the only good thing in that fabled container was hope. In their preoccupation with humans as dupes, they forget the power of hope, and the fact that we alone can experience and understand it. The pessimists have also lost touch with faith and love and what we are like at our best.

It is not surprising that moderns beat against the bars of the rational grid that technology and even some theology have clamped over their living space. The so called "New Age" has, among other things, revived astrology, searching again the numb and frozen stars for direction. But we are not made intelligible by the stars. Quite the reverse is true. The stars are made intelligible by our minds. They are charted on the map that issues from human intelligence.

To the confounding of Galileo, the human person, not the sun, is the center of the universe, dominating creation, teasing out its secrets and working its energy to good purposes. Cynics and critics forget the place of persons in the scheme of things, and so they have also forgotten their promise and their possibilities.

It has been said that at one point in their history the Greeks turned to the stars for direction because it was easier to surrender to them than to accept responsibility for themselves. We are at that point again; we can be overwhelmed by the burden of our errors, or we can take charge of ourselves and our destiny once more. Believers cannot choose fatalism and despair. The greatest reality for them is that they live at the center of a redeemed universe and the Spirit, not the stars, is the source of their strength.

Persons, scarred by violence and war, confused by the pain of so much of their own experience, are trying to remember what they are really like. They seem as innocent children who have learned too much, longing for the strengths they seemed to have in simpler times. People of faith cannot stand around weeping for themselves and their children as they look for the Lord in the skies. They are responsible for the human family and for sharing with its members the eternal freshness of the Gospels. The word "Gospel," it must be remembered, means good news.

In the twenty-fifth chapter of St. Matthew, the saved, in the setting of the Last Judgment, ask the Lord, "When did we see you hungry and feed you; or thirsty and give you drink? When did we see you a stranger and make you welcome; naked and clothe you; sick or in prison and go to see you?" There is a contemporary answer to that. It is the now generation that hungers and thirsts for an understanding of themselves and their place in the panorama of creation. They are strangers in the double-grip of loneliness and alienation; naked, when exposed to a punishing and contrary world; sick when they have lost touch with their wholeness; in prison when they are bound by superstition and inhuman philosophies of life.

In a world where things are made to wear out, people are searching for the things that last. Good men and women, lost for the moment in their tortured journeyings, not only need but want an understanding of the basics of faith, hope, and love. These are the interpersonal virtues, the ones that touch the most valued and basic experiences of their lives. Faith, hope, and love give us life, the measure of our meaning, and the fulfillment of our longings for the spiritual. Although their source is the Spirit, these things that last are found only in our relationships with each other. Life is lived with each other or it isn't lived at all.

With all their well-documented faults and missteps, humans alone, of all created things, are the instruments through which the Spirit transforms the face of the earth. Religion, then, is centered in the struggle of humans to believe even when they can be betrayed, to hope even when they can be disappointed, and to love even when they can be hurt in the effort.

We reach into space but we can also reach into ourselves. We are not likely to succeed in either endeavor if we look only at the bad news, blame others for our problems, or surrender to the sway of the stars, the glint of crystals, or some other passive solution. Our fulfillment comes from our commitment to the good news, not to keep it to ourselves, but to share it with abused but lovable human beings.

Chapter 62

A THANKSGIVING PRAYER

T HE GOOD THINGS for which we thank God are stacked like the autumn harvest in our hearts. If we are grateful for all that is good, we may also thank God for things that seem bad. At this last rise before winter, as we brace ourselves against cold and dark no one can predict, we may thank God that we can feel pain and know sadness, for these are the human sentiments that constitute our glory as well as our grief.

Were we to purge these from our lives, as some try to through a variety of escapes, we would also lose the experiences from which our joy and happiness flow. We would never feel loss in our relationships unless we first knew love. So, too, the terrible feeling of missing someone is the resonation within us of having first succeeded in being close to another human being. Blessed are they who can cry, for their tears attest to their having lived deeply enough to know the meaning of separation and sorrow. For tears shed from love, we thank the Lord.

We are grateful, too, that we bear these scars that are the proof that we have said yes to life, that we are, in the words of psychiatrist Harry Stack Sullivan, much more simply human than anything else. And for that gift of God, in which joy outweighs all pain, we are grateful at Thanksgiving and on every day of the year.

Chapter 63

BEYOND OUR BROKENNESS

A S WITH MOST SIGNALS about the mysteries of existence, Fermilab's proton accelerator lies, largely unnoticed, in plain sight, as if it had grown naturally out of the rich black plains thirty miles west of Chicago. Within the curl of the earthwork berm that rides the accelerator like an ocean swell, buffalo graze and swans glide on the waters that cool the electromagnets. The administration tower is set like a fine stone in the earthen ring.

The complex is a spiritual twin to France's Beauvais Cathedral whose proportions it borrowed along with its function of evoking and pointing beyond everyday mystery. At the main entrance soaring as boldly as a church cross is a sculpture of steel arches titled "Broken Symmetry."

This symbolizes the physicists' intuition that a symmetrical universe can only be imagined because we observe its unfinished signature in the asymmetry of this one, that we may imagine a perfect world on the evidence of the imperfect one daily spread about us. The promise of unbrokenness lifts off its brokenness as hope does from the crib of a newborn. Our faulted world abounds, as Timothy Ferris suggests, with "rumors of perfection."*

We search for symmetry beyond our own brokenness. Looking at life's scattered shards of beauty we imagine the wholeness from which they were born like stars flecked out of a perfect galaxy. Stretched on time's rack, we catch a fleeting vision of a universe in which we are free of the sadnesses of aging, illness, misunderstanding, and death sown into its passage. We dream of eternity in which we are struck free of its chains and find ourselves in that perfect place prophesied in every one of life's imperfections.

When we moan that there is no justice in this world, or that someone never has good luck or a real chance at life, or that all

---

*Timothy Ferris, *Coming of Age in the Milky Way* (New York: Anchor, Doubleday, 1988), 302.

others know is deformity or pain, or that some carry nothing while others bear every burden, we make a claim on the unbroken pattern, as of a glowing rose window, whose promise gleams in every scattered piece of stained glass.

Our basic yearning for wholeness is the defining pain of being human, the suffering that separates us from every other species, wrenching out the stuff of our common mystery as the Fermi accelerator does that of the universe — "our" pain as is no other. We may look beyond it, but we cannot get beyond it. This pain, in its thousand ordinary manifestations, goes along with being human. It tells us that we are human. We would know neither ourselves nor each other without it.

Examining this pain, we realize that it resembles a torn ticket, that it is the other half of that which admits us to life's glories. In the pain of being human we feel what is unfinished in ourselves. In this half life, however, we also experience that which makes us whole. We love and can be loved, we trust and can be trusted, we bestow hope and have it invested in us only because of our essential imperfection. These are dangerous experiences, almost sure to go wrong in larger or smaller ways, yet, missing them we miss life itself.

This book is ended but it is not complete. It has only made a beginning at its subject, fortunate if all it suggests is that our torn ticket is still valid for entrance into the central mysteries of living. These are not exotic but ordinary, available in abundance everywhere, hidden in plain sight every day. Nor is there a time limit on our ticket. We can even get in, as most of us do, after the performance has started. You can still follow the story.

We may find ourselves sitting next to each other at the Last Judgment. We will be surprised, as the saved always are, to find through what ordinary experiences we earned our glory. How plain the human mysteries will sound as they are read aloud, just things we had a chance to do every day for each other and for strangers. We are saved by accepting the pain of being human, recognizing it in others, and responding to them undramatically and unselfconsciously.

We will end up at this Last Judgment finding that we are not dressed for it, maybe a little late, and that we are hardly ready to appear in public, much less before a heavenly tribunal. Yet that is the condition in which we save ourselves: never at our best, always less than perfect but rising at moments — that may be the wrong ones for us but the right ones for others — by being human to them without worrying about its costs or pains. In such moments we reach that fullness of ourselves that depends on but also transcends our imperfection. We glimpse the symmetry implicit in that brokenness, the eternal that in turn breaks itself open to those who feel its pain but never let it stop them from being human anyway.